SAILOR
A PICTORIAL HISTORY

SAILOR
A PICTORIAL HISTORY

Alan McGowan

Life on board the world's
fighting ships from the
beginnings of photography
to the present day

Macdonald and Jane's
London

Copyright © Roxby Press Productions Limited 1977
All rights reserved, including the right to reproduce
this book, or parts thereof, in any form

First Published in Great Britain in 1977 by
Macdonald & Jane's Publishers Limited
Paulton House, 8 Shepherdess Walk
London N1 7LW

Made by Roxby Press Productions Limited
98 Clapham Common North Side, London SW4 9SG

ISBN 0354 01126 X

Editor   Christopher Chant
Design   Hillman Rainbird
Production   Reynolds Clark Associates Limited
Picture Research   Philippa Lewis
Filmset by Rembrandt Filmsetting Limited

Printed and bound in Spain
by TONSA, San Sebastián, and RONER, S. A., Madrid
D. L.: S. S. 487-1977

CONTENTS

CHAPTER 1

PRE-1914

The story of modern naval development is not the story of any one navy; rather it will be found in the struggle for supremacy of countries for which a large and powerful naval force was judged to be a vital necessity.

Rarely had any one of these countries the prolonged advantage of sole possession of either a new weapon or a breakthrough in technology. The pacemakers in the naval power game were those nations for whom a strong navy was either a geographical requirement or a political expedient.

In the middle of the nineteenth century, when photography became a practical medium for recording events, the two leading navies of the world were those of Britain, pre-eminent since 1805, and France, her ancient adversary. The photographs in this book are the chronicle of a revolution already begun, a revolution which would change the naval scene across the world. In shipbuilding the metal hull and the screw-propelled steamship had already appeared, and these innovations would shortly be applied to warship development; it was only a matter of time before the steam engine was developed to the stage where sails

Left: **The Spanish sail training corvette *Villa de Bilbao.***
Above: **Four old hands reminisce on board the US Navy's steam corvette *Mohican.***

could be discarded entirely, and steel could be produced sufficiently cheaply for it to replace iron as the chief shipbuilding material, though iron itself had only recently displaced the traditional wood.

During the succeeding sixty years the world's navies underwent a remarkable change. Any sailor who had taken part in the great sea battles of the seventeenth century would have felt at home aboard the ships of the line at the time of the Crimean War (1854-56), for all that several of them had auxiliary machinery with screw propellers. Had the reincarnation taken place fifty years later, the sailor would have been lost in the maze of new technology.

In the absence of any major war, the second half of the nineteenth century was, in British terms, a period of rising prosperity. The change in shipbuilding from sail and wood to steam and steel gave Great Britain an advantage over her rivals, since heavy industry was already well organised and able to expand rapidly. But in every country prepared to finance a navy, the growth of industrial technology resulted in new ideas in every aspect of naval construction.

The evolution of warship design had progressed slowly enough since the introduction of steam engines and paddle wheels in the smallest vessels in the 1820s. A quarter of a century later, the screw-propeller, less vulnerable and more efficient than the paddle wheel, had proved itself superior for naval purposes; and proposals had been made in the navies of both France and Britain for ships built of iron.

The Crimean War provided the spark that galvanised the innately conservative navies of Great Britain and France into life. Both were criticised for remaining obstinately conservative at times during the second half of the century, but all the same many radical steps were taken, and the moves and countermoves in the duel inspired other nations to join the experimental and development race. Italy contributed sporadically, following her emergence as a unified state; the United States of America was among the first in the field, but then lapsed into two decades of lethargy following the Civil War of 1861-65; Prussia, with a small navy, but with technically advanced and highly organised steel and armaments industries, was immediately able to lead the German empire to the forefront of naval development. Japan came late into the naval armaments race, but having joined, rapidly became a major seapower.

During the Crimean War the destructive power of shells (hollow rounds filled with explosive) amply demonstrated the need for armour, the value of which was later proved by floating batteries so protected. As a result the *Gloire,* a wooden frigate with iron armour plating, and capable of attacking with impunity a large number of conventional ships of the line, was launched by France in 1859. However, the British Admiralty had also learned the lesson of the Crimean War and in 1860 launched the far more revolutionary *Warrior,* iron hulled and armoured, at that time the largest and most powerful warship ever built.

Following the success of the *Warrior,* guns became heavier and armour became thicker to withstand them. The armour of 1860 had consisted of $4\frac{1}{2}$-inch (114.3mm) wrought iron plates backed by teak. By the time the British *Inflexible* (1876) and the French *Admiral Duperré* (1879) were built, their thickest armour plate was of 24 inches (609.6mm) and 22 inches (558.8mm) respectively.

By this time a new state, Italy, had entered the lists and built the *Duilio* (1876) using steel as armour for the first time. Iron was used in the *Admiral Duperré.*

The construction of the *Inflexible* and the *Duilio* illustrates how national rivalry forced development. The Italians originally intended to mount 35-ton (35,562kg) guns but on being told that the manufacturers were prepared to supply 60-ton (60,963kg) guns, accepted the heavier weapons. It had been intended to mount guns of 60 tons in the *Inflexible,* but learning of the change in the *Duilio's* armament, the British fitted her with 80-ton (81,285kg) guns. The Italians promptly adopted 100-ton (101,606kg) guns for the *Duilio.*

To pierce the ever-increasing thickness of armour, the elongated shell with an ogival head (the type still used) was developed in the mid-1860s. By means of studs on the shell (for muzzle-loaders) or a driving band at the base (for breech-loaders) the new pointed shells fired from rifled barrels attained greater accuracy and penetrating power.

The French produced an efficient breech-loading gun which was adopted in 1867; and in Germany, after something of a false start, Krupp breech-loaders were adopted in 1868.

An early result of the increasing weight of guns was the inevitable reduction in the number of such weapons that could be carried. To counter this disadvantage, they were fitted on revolving mountings called turrets or, a variation, barbettes, which made the guns more effective by increasing their arcs of fire. Both armour and turret were proved effective when the Federal *Monitor* met the Confederate *Merrimac* in 1862 during the American Civil War.

The greatest obstacles to the efficient use of the gun turret were the masts and rigging, at that time still considered an essential auxiliary to a major sea-going warship. The first vessel to be freed of these encumbrances was the British *Devastation* (1871). Not yet convinced of the mechanical reliability of pure steamships, the French navy deliberately retained sail for another decade.

Early steam engines were inefficient, largely because of the very limited boiler pressures available, but the reintroduction of the surface condenser and the development of the compound engine in the 1860s led to more power and larger ships in the mid-1870s.

Just when it seemed that the point had been reached when the maximum amount of armour was being carried, though it was still penetrable by certain guns, improved technology made mass-produced high quality steel available. By1884 the Creusot works in France, pioneers of steel armour, had produced plates which left all other armour far behind. The mass production of steel permitted the construction of larger vessels, the propulsion of which was now a practical proposition with the introduction of the triple expansion engine and multiple screws.

It was about this time, in the 1880s, that the USA emerged from her Rip van Winkle-like slumber and began to build a new navy. As it happened she had lost little, since the introduction of steel on a large scale and the new powerful engines and guns were about to create a revolution within a revolution.

The evolution of the battleship, which was designed to dominate decisive fleet actions, was accompanied by the evolution of the cruiser for trade defence, commerce-raiding, patrol and scouting duties. The problems were very similar to those of the major units—the difficulty of reconciling the conflicting claims of speed, endurance, armour and firepower.

New weapons also appeared. During the Crimean

War Russia had introduced moored mines, then called torpedoes. In 1870 the locomotive or self-propelled torpedo was introduced into the British navy and was quickly adopted by others. The fish-torpedo, as it was often called, was invented by a Captain Luppis of the Austro-Hungarian navy and perfected by Robert Whitehead, an English engineer then working in Fiume. The development of improved versions was rapid and the consequences enormous. For the first time, a single projectile was capable of sinking a battleship, and thought had to be given to armour below the waterline. Torpedo boats, at first provided with no armament other than torpedoes, then emerged, their relatively high speeds making them potentially very dangerous.

The speed and size of torpedo boats made them difficult targets for the guns of the day. This led to the adoption of the Gatling and Maxim type of machine-gun for the defence of large vessels. At the same time larger torpedo boats, armed with guns as well as torpedoes, were built to fulfil the dual role of torpedo boat and torpedo boat destroyer, or just destroyer.

The torpedo was developed for use from the torpedo boat, but it found its ideal carrier in the submarine. Although experiments with submersibles date back to the eighteenth century, the first practical submarines did not appear until the 1880s. France and the United States introduced their own versions at the turn of the century, closely followed by Britain and Italy. Germany did not build submarines until 1906.

The last major development of the nineteenth century relevant to warships was the marine steam turbine produced in 1897. Within two years the first turbine-driven British warship was in commission, and other countries rapidly followed suit.

At about the same time the major navies of the world began using oil as fuel. The advantages of oil over coal were numerous: it increased a ship's radius of action by about 40 per cent, the stokehold force could be reduced by 55 per cent, it permitted far more rapid increases of steam pressure, and refuelling was faster, simpler and, to the crew's delight, cleaner.

The Italian navy was the first to use oil, following the successful invention of a satisfactory burner in 1890. Although torpedo boats were fitted to burn oil alone, for some years the larger ships burned it in conjunction with coal. Germany and France adopted mixed combustion in the 1890s, Great Britain in the early years of the twentieth century. The United States did not consider the matter until 1904, but the investigating board then recommended that oil alone should be used.

In August 1914 no capital ship used oil fuel alone, the first such being the vessels of the *Queen Elizabeth* class and the *Oklahoma* class, laid down in 1912 by Great Britain and the United States respectively.

In naval terms three momentous events occurred in the twentieth century before the outbreak of war in 1914. First, the invention of wireless, hard on the heels of the adoption of the morse code and the electric signal lamp, revolutionised signalling, which for nearly two centuries had been solely visual and implemented by flags. Second, the production by Britain of the *Dreadnought*, launched in 1906, astounded the world. Turbine-driven, and therefore fast, yet heavily armed and as heavily armoured, she immediately rendered all existing battleships obsolete. The type was immediately copied and within three years similar vessels had been launched by Germany, France and the USA.

The third development was not strictly on the sea at all: it may be thought ironic that almost two years before the *Dreadnought* was laid down, the first flights were being made by the vehicle that ultimately spelled the end to all battleships: the aeroplane.

The position of Germany as a relative latecomer was in some respects similar to that of the United States. Traditionally a continental power, Prussia and the states which made up the German empire were unwilling to finance a very expensive navy until the arousal of great anti-British sentiment during the Boer War, an experience which seared the soul of Germany because the British navy prevented her from following words with deeds. One result of the Jameson Raid in 1896, the event that sparked off the war, was immediate support for the Navy Bills of Admiral von Tirpitz and Kaiser Wilhelm II in 1897 and 1900. With her background of armament technology Germany became a major naval power within five years.

It was suggested at the time that the British Admiralty was wrong to introduce the *Dreadnought*, thereby at a stroke discounting the preponderance of pre-dreadnought battleships enjoyed by the British navy. But such an argument not only presupposed that the secret could have been kept for a long time, which was impossible, but also that naval architects in other countries were incapable of producing a similar design independently, which was highly unlikely.

In fact other countries, notably the United States of America and Italy, were already considering the construction of battleships of the same type when the *Dreadnought* was laid down in 1905. By taking the decision to build the *Dreadnought*, which was completed in 1906, Britain gained a three year lead, for it was 1909 before the first such battleships appeared in the navies of Britain's closest rivals, Germany and the United States. By the end of that year, Britain had seven dreadnoughts. with nine building, Germany two with eleven building, and the United States two with four building.

In August 1914 Britain's lead was still of considerable proportions.

Left, top: The Commander-in-Chief, Channel Squadron, with his second-in-command and his captains, 1895-96. The C-in-C, Vice-Admiral Lord Walter Kerr, stands in the centre; in front of him, seated, is Rear-Admiral A. H. Alington; seated at the extreme right of the picture is Vice-Admiral Lord Kerr's flag-captain, Captain Arthur Barrow, RN, of HMS *Majestic*; standing, second from right is Captain C. J. Barlow, DSO, RN, of the *Magnificent,* flag captain to Rear-Admiral Alington.

Left, bottom: Looking even less relaxed, in their studied casualness, officers of the USS *Monitor* pose in front of the turret on 9 July 1862, three months after the famous action with Confederate *Merrimac* in Hampton Roads, Virginia.

Right: On board the Danish Royal Yacht *Dannebrog* in 1902, the crew of the royal barge poses in front of the starboard paddle-box with the petty officer coxwain in the centre.

Below: Russian sailors, c1902. Complete with boat-hooks and paddles, they are clearly a boat crew.

Overleaf: In 1872 an expedition sponsored by the British government and organised by the Royal Society and the University of Edinburgh left Portsmouth in HMS *Challenger*. The aim was to chart the depths and record the movement of the seas and the life within them, to record the presence of whatever minerals might be found and to record climatic phenomena. In a highly successful voyage that lasted over three years the ship covered 68,000 miles (109,440km). The *Challenger,* under the command of Captain George Nares, was a wooden hulled square-rigged sailing vessel with auxiliary steam engines. Some of the *Challenger*'s men are here pictured with young friends in the Philippine Islands.

13

Left: Trainee stokers receive elementary instruction into the mysteries of big-ends and con-rods in a triple expansion engine on board the battleship HMS *Nelson* in 1910. The cleared mess-deck is being used as a classroom, but at meal-times the tables will be set up again. The hooks above the arms rack and the bars suspended from the deckhead are for slinging hammocks. This is one of the stokers' messes, of which the class in the picture forms a very small part.

Below: Cutlass exercise aboard the protected cruiser USS *Chicago* in 1898. To the right of the picture may be seen the forward port 8-inch (203mm) gun.

Bottom: In the stokehold of HMS *Nelson,* stokers re-lay bricks over a firebox under a watchful eye of a petty officer. Launched in 1906 and completed two years later, the *Nelson* was the last pre-dreadnought built for the Royal Navy. She was also the last capital ship fitted with reciprocating steam engines. Her fuel was coal (2,000 tons maximum) and oil (400 tons).

15

Top: Royal Navy reservists clean an 8-inch (203mm) rifled muzzle-loading gun aboard HMS *Firefly* under the supervision of a Regular petty officer during their annual drill in 1876. Each gun had to cover as wide an arc as possible because the enormous weight limited the number of guns that could be carried. The guns were mounted on rollers which ran on iron tracks fastened to the deck. The rings to which the gun tackles were hitched to move it can be seen on the right, near the rammer and other equipment. To avoid marking the holystoned and scrubbed deck the crew did not normally wear boots on board.

Above: French sailors pose with 100mm (3.9-inch) QF (quick-firing) guns aboard a training cruiser, c1911. The 'shields' are wooden mock-ups. Note the fixed ammunition, that is with cartridge and projectile together as one unit. Fixed ammunition was one of the means used to increase the rate of fire. The sailor second from the left, in the foreground, is holding a shell removed from its cartridge case for the purposes of demonstration.

Right: Two sailors of the Royal Norwegian Navy, c1890, demonstrate the use of the 6-pdr quick-firing gun on a low mounting at the stern of the gunboat *Tyr* (1888).

Left: Japanese sailors with an early breech-loading gun aboard a sloop or corvette in the 1880s. This gun, by no means the largest of its day, suggests some of the difficulties in handling and controlling such monsters before the days of hydraulics.

Above: Two petty officer instructors demonstrate the use of the Maxim machine-gun, mounted on a field carriage for use by landing parties. HMS *Excellent* is the name of the Royal Navy's Gunnery School on Whale Island in Portsmouth Harbour.

Right: Turkish officers and ratings pose with the guns on board a training ship, c1905. In the foreground is a 14-pdr field piece. In the background is a 6-inch Krupp-built gun. In 1900 Turkey had seven battleships, of which the most modern was 15 years old. The average age of the remainder was 35 years. Largely under German tutelage the Turkish navy was reorganised and re-equipped. By 1914 it was a considerable force containing two modern dreadnoughts.

Below right: British stokers load rifles during arms 'drill' aboard a cruiser, c1910. That the petty officer in charge tolerated idlers watching suggests that the photograph was posed. Note the wheels of the 12-pdr field guns on the left, and the scrubbed hammocks hung out to dry in the sun.

Left: Aboard the Russian Royal Yacht *Almaz* (1903) during the Tsar's visit to Sebastopol in 1905, the captain tastes the soup served to the ratings.

Right: John Skon, reputedly the man who fired the first shot from the USS *Raleigh* (1892) in Manila Bay on 1 May 1898 at the start of the Spanish-American War.

Below right: Admiral Togo, the victorious Japanese commander-in-chief at the Battle of Tsushima in 1905. When Japan became westernised in the last decades of the nineteenth century it was because her rulers realised that Japan could only maintain her independence by being able to oppose the Western Powers with western weapons. With this in mind the army was reformed on Prussian lines and a modern navy was created, based on the Royal Navy. All its major warships and many lesser ones were designed and built in Britain. In the Russo-Japanese War of 1904-1905 the Russian Army was comprehensively defeated by an inferior Japanese force at Mukden. Even this might have been made good, though, but for Russia's overwhelming defeat at sea. The Japanese began the war, as they were later to begin another, by a surprise attack on the enemy fleet. Japanese destroyers descended upon the Russian fleet at Port Arthur in the very early hours of 8 February 1904. The result was not as successful as it might have been, but the two newest Russian battleships and a cruiser had been damaged and were out of action for some weeks. The first real battle, in the Yellow Sea, occurred when the Russian force tried to break through to the Russian port of Vladivostok. The flagship was eventually sunk by shell-fire but Admiral Vitgeft, the new commander-in-chief, was killed early in the battle. In all, the Russians lost the battleship *Tsarevitch* and three cruisers which, badly damaged, sought shelter in various treaty ports of China and were interned. Meanwhile the Russians had been preparing new ships to restore the situation. The fleet left the Baltic in October under Admiral Rozhestvensky. It was finally intercepted by Togo's force in the Straits of Tsushima. Rozhestvensky was outmanoeuvred by Togo, whose ships were more effective and crews' morale high. For the loss of a number of torpedo boats Togo sank six battleships, a coast defence ship and three cruisers. He captured the other two battleships, two coast defence ships and a destroyer.

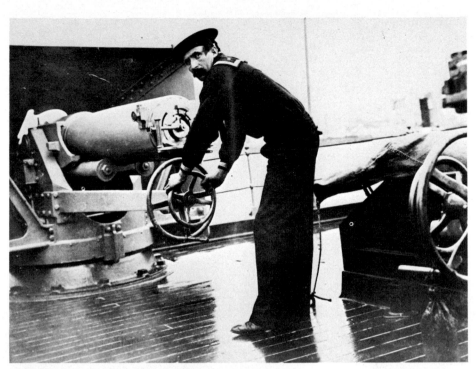

Left: The French *La Dévastation* (1879) is an excellent example of the battleship in the years immediately prior to the general introduction of the turret. As guns became larger and the armour to protect them became thicker, it was necessary to concentrate them in a 'central battery' or 'casemate' to get the most protection from the least weight of armour. The casemate was situated above the engine-room. *La Dévastation*'s main armament of four 12.6-inch (320mm) guns were sited one at each 'corner' of the casement. Her principal secondary armament, two 10.5-inch (270mm) guns, were in single barbettes on top of the casemate. The port 10.5-inch gun can be seen beneath the cantilevered wing of the bridge.

Right, above: The *Shikishima* (1898) was built at the Thames Ironworks, London, for the Imperial Japanese Navy. She was a good example of the older type of battleship made obsolescent by the *Dreadnought* in 1906. Her armament was typical of the pre-dreadnought: four 12-inch (305mm) guns, fourteen 6-inch (152.4mm) and twenty 3-inch (76.2mm)

Right, below: Three early French coast defence battleships at Cherbourg, c1875. Note the turrets armed with short muzzle-loading guns, and the ram bow. *Le Cerbère*, on the extreme left, was built at Brest in 1865. The ram was re-introduced as a naval weapon in modern times following the *Monitor-Merrimac* action of 1862. A sharp edge formed by toughened iron, later steel, located just below the waterline at the bow, the ram was meant as a ship-killer, as indeed it proved. Unfortunately, soon after the ram was adopted, the Battle of Lissa in the Austro-Italian War seemed to prove the effectiveness of the new weapon. The Austrian commander-in-chief, Admiral Tegetthof, drove his flagship at the *Ré d'Italia,* which sank like a stone immediately he backed away from the huge hole his ram had caused. Incredibly, the fact that the *Ré d'Italia* was stationary at the time was ignored. From Lissa until the end of the nineteenth century all warships of any consequence were built with a ram bow, but never again did it prove to be a significant weapon. During the approximately 35 years of its use, the ram sank two British ships, two Russian, two French, one Spanish and one German ship—all friendly ships sunk by accidental collision; against this can be set its sole success against a hostile ship.

Previous page: The Austrian battleship *Radetzky* (1909), 14,500 tons. A small battleship of the dreadnought type, the *Radetzky* was especially adapted for use in the shallow Adriatic Sea. An obvious element of the compromise is her mixed armament which can clearly be seen: four 12-inch (305mm) guns (bow and stern), eight 9.4-inch/240mm guns (the twin turrets are placed on each side of the masts) and twenty 4.1-inch (105mm) guns.

Right: German seamen prepare the midday meal aboard a cruiser, c1903.

Below: Danish seamen peel potatoes on board the coast defence battleship *Herluf Trolle* (1899) in the winter of 1906. It seems likely that the leading hand of their mess had decided that he was not going to have the litter of potato-peeling on the mess-deck. The arrangements for preparing and eating meals was much the same in the world's navies. In order to keep the size of the galley and the number of galley staff to a minimum, meals were prepared on the mess-deck by the members of the mess, and taken to the galley to be cooked. At meal-times it was collected by men from the mess.

Bottom: Officers enjoy after-dinner port in the wardroom of the British battleship *Sans Pareil* (1887) in 1899. On the right is an officer of the royal Marine Artillery. The comfort of the wardroom depended very much upon the financial circumstances of its members; before the First World War, most naval officers had a private income. The Royal Navy provided simple furniture, and food at the same basic cost per day per officer as for each rating.

Top: American sailors dance on the fo'c's'le of a *New Jersey* class battleship in the Hudson river on a sunny evening in 1911.

Centre: Sailors of the French battleship *Dévastation* (1879) at Toulon also relax in the evening sunshine on a Sunday a few years earlier. They have probably just returned from Mass since they are all in No 1 dress and the side drummer reading the newspaper still has his drum and sticks. The pastimes seem to be universal: reading, Housey-Housey (Bingo), cards and just watching.

Above: Cards by the midships torpedo-tube of the destroyer HMS *Seal* (1897).

Right: The participants in the Midsummer's Eve carnival on board the Norwegian *Kong Sverre* in 1902.

...ptog på Kong Sverre 1902

29

Left: British boy sailors line up for an issue of soap, each bar being ticked off in the ledger.

Top: Danish seamen wash their clothes on a quay near the stern of the *Sjaelland*. Launched in 1858 as a screw-frigate, the *Sjaelland* became an accommodation ship in 1885.

Above: For a sailor, washing clothes was a primitive affair. *Matelots* aboard the twenty-year old French battleship *Jauréguiberry* (1893), make the best of a poor situation.

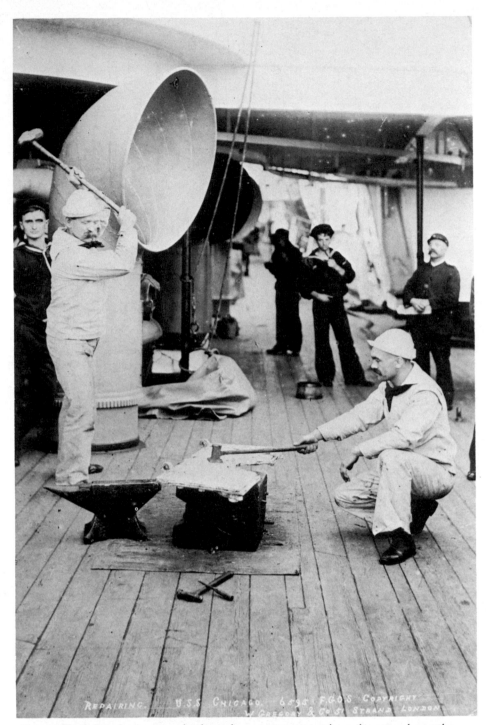

Above left: Sailmakers at work aboard a British warship. The rating with the three good conduct badges (stripes) is working on a new sail for one of the ship's boats, making eyelet holes with a marlin-spike. His bench has holes to make a handy rack for the tools. The rating (notice the bare feet) is making, or repairing, a chafing mat.

Left: Coaling ship in the Royal Navy, c1910. A tally-man is in the right background. Canvas has been rigged to protect paintwork from being chipped by carelessly handled shovels, barrows and sacks. The ship's company of a battleship could handle about 140 tons of coal per hour. Notice that the specially made bags, marked with the government broad arrow, have the attached rope handles going right round them for additional strength. The pipe of the man in the foreground will not be alight, but rather 'smoked' as a placebo.

Above: Blacksmiths on board the USS *Chicago* (1885) apparently repairing the upper port-lid of one of the midships battery (5-inch/127mm) gun ports. Behind the upraised hammer is the cowl of a ventilator which carried air down below decks, particularly to the engine room. The cowl could be turned to face into the wind. Contrary to British practice at that time, all the American sailors wore shoes on board as a normal practice.

Giovine Crispo

Above: A junior lieutenant in the engineering branch of the Italian navy. Only the executive branch had the curl on the gold lace stripe; the engineering branch wore black between the stripes.
Above right: A submarine diving class from HMS *Excellent* at Whale Island aboard their tender. The officer in charge is sitting on the thwart in the foreground. Although providing instruction for 'submarine classes', as diving training was called, HMS *Excellent* was still primarily the Royal Navy's gunnery school and incongruous though it may seem under the circumstances, the instructor standing on the gunwale still wears the high gaiters that are the Whale Island 'trademark'.
Right: This group of young Italian sailors are standing round one of the six 4.7-inch (120mm) guns aboard the training ship *Cristoforo Colombo* (1875) at about the turn of the century.

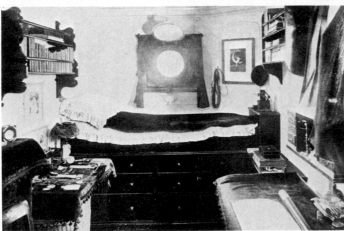

Far left: Captain Churchill of the battleship HMS *Nile* (1888) is piped aboard at Malta in 1898. On deck to receive him is the Midshipman of the Watch.

Above: Captain the Hon H. Lambton's cabin aboard the cruiser HMS *Powerful* (1895), on the China Station in 1898. Such a cabin reflected the private means of the occupant as well as his personal taste, for the furniture provided by the navy was, understandably, fairly basic. It is not surprising that it appears very like a well-to-do bachelor's apartment ashore, for family man though he was, at sea Captain Lambton was of course very much a bachelor. The type of plants shown were typical cabin, as well as civilian, decoration of the day.

Left: A lieutenant's cabin on board the battleship HMS *Anson* (1886) on the Mediterranean Station in 1897. It is essential that so small a cabin should be kept tidy, but the navigating lieutenant, Arthur Hayes-Sadler, was obviously meticulously neat. Only the bare essentials were provided by the navy. The tablecloths and bed covers would have been the occupant's personal property, as would have been the books, photograph on the wall and other private effects.

Top: Cutlass drill on the quarterdeck of HMS *Resolution*: an anachronism by this time, for no one seriously supposed men would be sent to board a hostile warship in the old Nelsonic tradition. Nevertheless the drill doubtless had some value as physical exercise. Around the edge of the barbette is stowed the steel torpedo net.

Above: When a sailor died, all his immediate personal effects were returned to his next-of-kin and his uniform was auctioned among his messmates, the proceeds also being sent to his next-of-kin. In the picture, the Master-at-Arms is acting as auctioneer while a Writer records the successful bids. Among the spectators are two petty officers, two marines (RMA and RMLI) and, in the lower right hand corner, the Divisional Officer of the dead man.

Right: More orthodox physical training is carried out on the fo'c's'le of HMS *Howe* (1885) with bars and barbells. Once the Medical Officer had pronounced a man fit, his physical well-being, with that of the rest of the ship's company, was in the care of the 'lieutenant responsible (among other things) for physical training duties'. In this he was aided and abetted indirectly by the Gunnery Officer and his Gunner's Mates whose dream was to make every ship a miniature *Excellent*.

Right: Pay day aboard HMS *Royal Sovereign* in 1895. The Paymaster places the pay of the rating (in this case a Petty Officer 1st Class) on the paychest. The recipient scoops it on to the top of his cap and checks it. Assisting the Paymaster is a Petty Officer Writer, whilst to one side the Master-at-Arms checks the rating's name in his book. Just out of the picture on the left, stands the Commander—the end of his telescope and his right hand can just be seen. The money was made up by the Paymaster's staff and each man's pay was placed in the correct order in one of the compartments in a drawer which was then slid into the chest for carrying to wherever payment was to be made. It will be seen from the petty officer's right hand that the men have been called from work, to which they will return immediately they have been paid and checked off.

Below: On board the cruiser HMS *Calliope* (1884) in 1890, a Royal Marine barber is at work. A Petty Officer 2nd Class leans on the breech of a 5-inch gun awaiting his turn.

Bottom. On the fo'c'sle of HMS *Howe,* the Paymaster Commander keeps a careful eye on the issue of duty free leaf tobacco.

CHAPTER 2

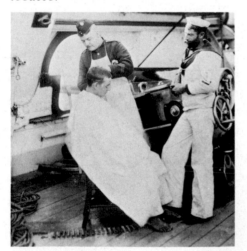

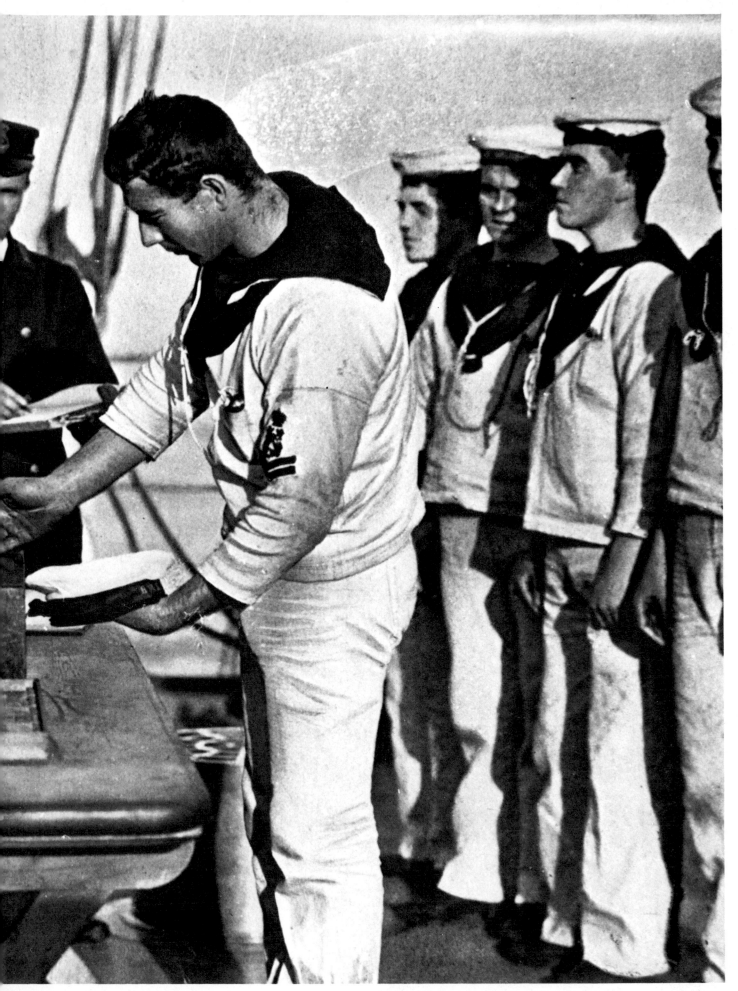

1914-1918

The rapid expansion of the German navy defeated the British aim that the Royal Navy should at all times be equal to that of any other two powers combined. By August 1914, in terms of capital ships, the German navy alone was two-thirds the size of that of Britain.

The determination of Kaiser Wilhelm II to challenge Britain's domination of the seas had been a major factor in the British government's decision to end its increasingly hazardous policy of 'splendid isolation'. Since from the British viewpoint the chief danger seemed now to come from Imperial Germany, it was natural that the government should seek some form of reconciliation with France, whose hatred of Germany, kindled in the humiliations of the Franco-Prussian War in 1870, burned no less fiercely thirty years later. Determined efforts in both Paris and London led eventually to the *Entente Cordiale* of April 1904, a rapprochement that led to military and naval 'talks'.

Blockade was the keystone of the naval strategy of both Britain and Germany, blockade under which the war effort of the other would wither and die.

Dependent as she was on imported foodstuffs and raw materials, Britain's very existence relied upon her control of the seas; that same supremacy also provided her with the means to impose a blockade upon her enemies. Imperial Germany was in a rather different position. Blockade by sea posed no immediate threat to her existence unless she were also opposed, even surrounded, by hostile nations on the continent of Europe. The German navy was not originally conceived as a threat to Britain, but rather as a means of affording Germany a freedom of action overseas denied her as long as the British navy's predominance was so overwhelming. Unfortunately, Wilhelm II could not, or would not, see that a navy far in excess of Germany's requirements could be seen by Great Britain only as a direct threat, since so large a navy was not necessary to her continued existence.

The sea war, in which Britain inevitably played the greatest part, took two forms: the containing of enemy warships in port, together with the elimination of any units already at sea; and the establishment of an economic blockade to prevent any goods which might sustain his war effort from reaching the enemy.

Because in the former, the counter-blockade, lay the key to all the naval tactics throughout the war, it is simpler to deal with the British economic blockade first. With the exception of a period in the submarine war in 1917, the British navy dominated the oceans of

Left: **Recruit trumpeters at the US Navy Sea Training Station, West Seattle, Washington.**
Above: **Royal Navy Reservists in August 1914.**

the world and within a few months German colonies were isolated from the 'Fatherland', with little possibility of succour, to be taken at leisure by the Allies.

After the first year of the war, a liberal interpretation of the term 'contraband' was drastically reduced by the British government, so that in the long run nearly all seaborne trade with the Central Powers (Germany and her allies) was stopped. It was not to be supposed that neutral powers would look with any favour upon the interruption of their commerce, even though Germany was doing the same thing by increasingly more ruthless means.

The British navy's attempts to combat the German blockade led to most of the major naval actions of the war. In 1914, the submarine was little more than a dozen years old as an effective warship, an unknown quantity whose menace was more potential than real. The immediate concern of the Allies, therefore, was to round up the German warships known to be be at sea, and to prevent their being joined by other units of the German navy. Given the preponderance of the Allied navies, the eventual elimination of the enemy commerce-raiders was only a matter of time, and in fact the French navy began by sinking the Austrian light cruiser *Zenta* in the Mediterranean on 16 August 1914. Nevertheless, during the first few months of the war, the five cruisers at large took a heavy toll of Allied merchant shipping, the exploits of the *Karlsruhe* in the Atlantic and the *Emden* in the Indian Ocean being the most notable.

The biggest actions outside northern waters were those involving Admiral Graf Spee's Pacific squadron. In November 1914, off Coronel in Chile, *Scharnhorst, Gneisenau, Leipzig* and *Nürnberg* sank the British cruisers *Good Hope* and *Monmouth;* the light cruiser *Glasgow,* badly damaged, and the armed merchant ship *Otranto* escaped. Five weeks later, the boot was on the other foot. The battle-cruisers *Invincible* and *Inflexible,* despatched to deal with Spee's squadron, came up with the enemy off the Falkland Islands. Only the light cruiser *Dresden* made a temporary escape.

Meanwhile, the British Grand Fleet, with the exception of a powerful Channel Squadron, was concentrated at Scapa Flow, in the Orkney Islands, ready to forestall any attempt by major units of the High Seas Fleet to reach the Atlantic through the North Sea, their most likely route. Close blockade, in the style of the Napoleonic wars, was made impossible by the widespread use of mines; in the eyes of many in the British navy, however, this was no disadvantage, since the 'no man's land' of the North Sea might encourage the High Seas Fleet to try conclusions. This indeed it did. Having noted in earlier skirmishes Admiral Beatty's eagerness to get his battle-cruisers into action, the German Commander-in-Chief,

Admiral Scheer, planned that Admiral Hipper's cruisers and battle-cruisers should trail their coat in the hope of leading a major portion of the British Grand Fleet on to the full might of the High Seas Fleet.

On the day, Hipper was completely successful, partly because of his tactical skill, but also because it suited Beatty's orders from the British Commander-in-Chief, Admiral Jellicoe. British intelligence had warned Jellicoe of the large German force at sea, and the battle-cruisers were to draw the unsuspecting High Seas Fleet on to the main battle fleet. The ensuing action, fought largely between the battle-cruisers of each fleet on 31 May 1916, became known as the Battle of Jutland, or, to the Germans, of the Skagerrak.

When Scheer found that Beatty's battle-cruisers were not a lone patrolling force, but were the van of the Grand Fleet, he realised that he was outnumbered, and turned away in order to avoid being cut off from his base. Thereafter a series of disconnected actions between the respective light forces took place during the hours of darkness and until some time after dawn the next day.

The first salvoes from the battle-cruisers were fired at 1548, and Scheer finally broke off the action at 1915. In the three and a half hour battle, the main battle fleets were in action twice, on each occasion for a matter of minutes only. Severe though the losses were on each side, the battle was really the initial skirmish between scouting forces as a prelude to the fleet action, which Scheer avoided. The material results must be regarded as a tactical victory for Scheer, whose fleet had sunk three battle-cruisers, three cruisers and eight destroyers for the loss of one battle-cruiser, one pre-dreadnought battleship, four cruisers and five destroyers. The damage inflicted on those German ships which regained the safety of the Jade Roads was considerable, for the German ships had sustained 121 hits from major projectiles as opposed to 55 hits on the British ships. There is no doubting the excellence of the German armour, but the chief reason why the German ships could take such punishment and still remain afloat was that they were deliberately designed with a far greater number of watertight compartments than their British counterparts.

Each of the three British battle-cruisers that were lost, however, sank within minutes of being hit, the reason in each case being a devastating internal explosion caused by the imperfect isolation of turrets from magazines, which made the latter vulnerable to any fire or flash caused by a hit on a turret.

The manoeuvres of Scheer and Hipper were exemplary. But if Beatty's handling of the British battle-cruisers was bold, Jellicoe has been castigated for being too cautious. In reality, however, the onus on each of the respective commanders-in-chief was quite different. If Scheer had suffered a major defeat it would have had little real consequence on the result of the war. On the other hand, if Jellicoe had suffered a major defeat, the way would have been open for German warships to destroy British shipping with impunity and bring the war to a very rapid conclusion. In Winston Churchill's words, Sir John Jellicoe was 'the only man on either side who could lose the war in an afternoon', and Jellicoe was only too well aware of the fact. In the event, the judgement of the British commander-in-chief was vindicated: he had not run any unnecessary risk, and the German fleet did not seek to renew the fight at any time during the remainder of the war.

In 1914 the potential menace of the submarine had quickly been translated into real terms. In September, little more than a month after the outbreak of war, the elderly armoured cruiser *Aboukir* was torpedoed by the submarine *U-9*. Her consorts were two of her sisterships, whose captains were no more attuned to this new factor in warfare than their colleagues in any navy in the world; instinctively, they both stopped to pick up survivors, but it was a humanitarian error against which subsequent captains learned to steel their hearts, for the *Cressy* and the *Hogue* were also torpedoed and sunk by the same submarine. A month later the first British merchant ship to fall victim to the submarine was sunk by the *U-17* off Norway.

The value of this new form of naval warfare was rapidly appreciated by the German high command. Although at the beginning of 1915 there were only twenty-seven U-boats in commission, with no real defence organised against them, this small but growing fleet soon made Britain the blockaded rather than the blockader.

However, the increasing use of submarine warfare brought sharp criticism from neutral countries whose citizens frequently fell victim to it. Until the Battle of Jutland the German government had vacillated over its submarine policy, but whatever the tactical result claimed, the events of 31 May 1916 convinced Germany that Britain's trans-oceanic lifeline was not to be broken by the surface forces. The construction of U-boats was given priority and the submarine war was increased to such an extent that in October 1916 176,000 tons of British shipping were sunk, together with nearly 75,000 tons sailing under the flags of other Allies and, most significant of all, 102,000 tons of neutral shipping.

Accepting the political risks, the German government declared its intention to wage unrestricted warfare from 1 February 1917 against all shipping within a so-called war zone extending around the British Isles and those coasts of Europe in the hands of the Allies. By the spring of 1917 there were severe shortages in Britain, and April saw the peak shipping losses: 881,000 tons. But two months of the new campaign brought the inevitable result and on 6 April 1917 the USA declared war on Germany.

The solution to submarine warfare had already been discovered, however. In the same month the convoy system, which had been begun in March for shipping between Britain and France, was extended to shipping from Scandinavia, and the first transatlantic convoy sailed in May. The results were immediate, and although Germany had its greatest number of U-boats in commission in October 1917, shipping losses continued to decline.

By 1918 some 3,000 Allied vessels were equipped with the newly developed hydrophones for picking up the sound of submerged submarines, and an effective depth-charge had also been produced. Anti-submarine barrages of nets and mines such as that laid across the Straits of Dover were only partially successful, as were the enormous minefields laid at the Atlantic exits of the North Sea. Attempts were also made to bottle up the U-boats in their bases: in April 1918 the sinking of blockships at Zeebrugge was successful, but a similar raid on Ostend failed at the first attempt and achieved only a limited success at the second. Aircraft were used for anti-submarine duties with increasing effect, but their range was very limited. Prior to 1917 only one U-boat was damaged by bombing. In 1917-18, eleven were sunk and thirty-one damaged by air patrols.

Inevitably we have been mainly concerned with the conflict between the titans, Britain and Germany, but the other nations on each side fulfilled such roles as were open to them. Austro-Hungarian submarines damaged the French battleship *Jean Bart* in 1914, and the entry of Italy into the war on the side of the Allies in 1915 led to much naval activity on the Adriatic. Neither side dominated that sea in 1915, although the Austro-Hungarian fleet, with the exception of its submarines, was confined to it, and was thus unable to play any part in the Mediterranean proper. The entry of the United States into the war in 1917 led to immediate reinforcement of the Allied navies. Within a month the first American destroyers arrived at Queenstown in Ireland for convoy duties. In December the United States' 6th Battle Squadron arrived at Scapa Flow, while three other battleships were based in Ireland for convoy duties against the possibility of surface-raiders breaking out into the Atlantic.

The story of naval warfare is usually one of action, as it must be, since decisions are rarely achieved by inaction. For the individual sailor, however, the war frequently consisted of long periods of boredom punctuated by brief spells of frenzied activity. This was as true for the sailor in the barracks in Wilhelmshaven or Pola as it was for the sailor landlocked by the bleak moors of the Orkneys. For those at sea it was usually a case of endless patrolling, with the excitement of any real action a rarity.

The most successful means of defence against U-boats was the convoy system, which resulted in a large number of enemy submarines being sunk by escort craft. Several U-boats were also sunk or damaged by mines laid to restrict their movement. Innocent-looking merchant ships with concealed guns and highly trained volunteer crews attempted to lure U-boats close. 'Panic crews' rushed for the boats and pulled away, to convince the raider that it was safe to close in, surfaced, for the kill. Then, as 'bulkheads' dropped, already aimed guns fired on the submarine at pointblank range. Another positive attack on U-boats was made in the spring of 1918 when, in a raid on Zeebrugge and Ostend, warships under Rear-Admiral Roger Keyes tried to seal the U-boat bases by sinking blockships at the harbour entrance. The raid on Zeebrugge was successful, but that at Ostend a failure, although a second raid achieved partial success.

Right: Some of the ship's company of the cruiser *Vindictive* (1897), Admiral Keyes's shell-scarred flagship, on her return from the raid.

Left, above: A Sopwith '1½-Strutter' is hoisted on to the launching platform on top of the after turret of HMS *Africa* (1905).

Left, below: Seamen from merchant ships sunk by the German armed merchant ship *Wolf* collect food on board at Kiel in February 1918.

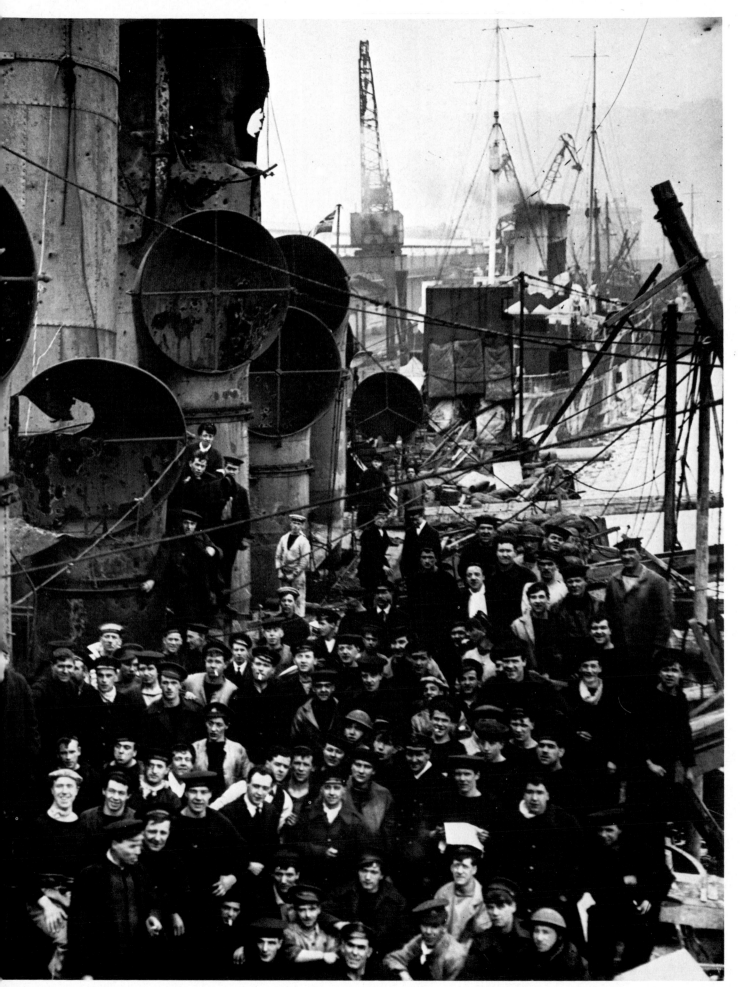

Far left: One of the aircrew from a German 'spotter' seaplane is helped aboard a U-boat.

Top: Greek seamen on board a sailing vessel are questioned about their activities by a British boarding party.

Above: American recruits pose on the barrel of a 12-inch (305mm) gun aboard a US battleship in 1917.

Left: After the loss of the British cruisers *Good Hope* (1898) and *Monmouth* (1900) at the Battle of Coronel, a force based on two battle-cruisers was sent to hunt the raiders, which were caught near the Falkland Islands and destroyed. Two marines survey some of the damage suffered aboard the light cruiser HMS *Kent* (1900) in the second action.

Top: A flotilla of small (150-ton) German torpedo boats in the Kiel Canal, c1914. Generally speaking, smaller vessels were identified by numbers, although destroyers were sometimes named. The torpedo boats in the background were four of a group of eight built by the Schichau company in 1889. Coal burners, with a maximum speed of 22 knots, they were each armed with three torpedo-tubes and a 4-pdr gun. They carried a complement of 24.

Above: The US Navy pre-dreadnought battleship *Kearsarge* had a main battery of four 13-inch (330mm) guns and a secondary battery of four superfiring 8-inch (203mm) guns.

Above right: Following the explosion of a mine attached to her hull by an Italian 'frogman', Commander Rosetti, the Austrian dreadnought *Viribus Unitis* is seen about to capsize and sink in Pola harbour. Men from the stricken ship can be seen in the water, and a boat from the vessel anchored nearby is already under way to pick up survivors. *Viribus Unitis* was the last of her class to be sunk in a six-month period that was disastrous for Austria-Hungary. The *Tegethoff* was torpedoed in Pola harbour in May 1918; in June, *Szent Istvan* and *Prinz Eugen* were sunk in the Adriatic Sea by Italian torpedo boats; *Viribus Unitis* was sunk in November.

Right: Part of the crew of a United States submarine.

On Saturday 7 October 1916, Hans Rose, one of the most successful U-boat commanders, sailed his *U-53* escorted by the US submarine *D2* into harbour at Newport, Rhode Island, ostensibly to deliver a confidential letter to the German ambassador. In fact the mission was part of a plan to demonstrate the ease with which U-boats could cross the Atlantic and operate in American waters. The mission, impudent but not particularly dangerous, was tactically a success; strategically, however, it was ill-conceived and misjudged the probable reaction. Having publicised his submarine's presence in the USA, Rose sailed well within the 24-hour time limit, but only as far as the Nantucket Shoal light vessel. There he sank five passing merchant ships. But long before British or Canadian warships could hope to arrive, *U-53* dipped her colours and submerged. Public opinion in the United States was, on the whole, shocked at the effrontery of the performance and was less impressed by the German navy than by the feeling that America might soon have to stop talking and act.

Far left: The officers and men of the *U-53* enjoy the peaceful autumn sunshine at Newport, Rhode Island in October 1916.

Above: Four members of the crew of a U-boat take the air in May 1918.

Left: A *matelot* emerges from the hatch of a French submarine in 1917.

Left, top: Admiral Sir David Beatty on the quarterdeck of his flagship HMS *Queen Elizabeth* with a visiting Brazilian admiral in 1918.

Left, centre: Seaman Pierrepoint Morgan Jun, the son of the American millionaire, with a 6-pdr QF gun on board a submarine-chaser.

Left, bottom: Kapitän Count von und zu Dohna-Schlodien, commander of the successful German raider *Moewe.*

Right: Fregatenkapitän Nerger and his men were feted on their return to Germany after the successful 15-month cruise of the auxiliary cruiser *Wolf.* With Nerger are, from left to right in greatcoats, General von Richthoven, General von Bonin, General von Kessel and (behind Nerger's shoulder) Admiral von Koch. Although the commerce-raiders, both warships and armed merchant ships, which had been at sea in August 1914 were eventually sunk, raiders of the latter type were a nuisance almost until the end of the war. The *Moewe* sank fifteen Allied and neutral ships on her first voyage under Dohna-Schlodien in 1915. On her second cruise, the *Moewe* sank six vessels before, harried by a naval squadron for whom she proved too fast, she was brought safely back to Wilhelmshaven again. If the *Seeadler*, another lone raider, was less successful, her captain achieved some fame for the gallantry towards and his solicitude for his prisoners. Of a different attitude was Karl Nerger of the aptly named armed merchant ship raider *Wolf.* The *Wolf* included among her victims four British hospital ships. Despite Nerger's practice of taking entire complements of passengers and crew aboard, nearly a hundred already sick or wounded men were lost from these ships. Altogether, in a voyage of some 64,000 miles (103,000 km), *Wolf* despatched 150,000 tons of Allied and neutral shipping before returning to Germany and a hero's welcome for her crew.

Speed, commensurate with her size, is a pre-requisite for any warship; and speed means high fuel consumption. The amount of coal required in a battleship in 1914 was enormous simply because the engines, like the ships, were huge. For example, the 23,000-ton battleship USS *Utah* (1909) had twelve boilers, and in her furnaces a grate area of 1,428 square feet. She normally carried 1,667 tons of coal, but in wartime her maximum amount of coal was 2,500 tons. Because a warship must be ready for service at any time, coaling ship was always the first job on returning to harbour. As in most navies, in the Royal Navy it was a job for all hands. To promote keenness and speed there was always a competition on board to see which team moved the most coal, and often there was a fleet competition. Once started, the job went on nonstop except for very brief 'stand-easy spells'. When the last bag of coal had been emptied there would be one more brief spell before the pipe 'Hands to Clean Ship', when all would turn-to and rid first the ship and then the person of the dust that seemed to have permeated everything. There was then, of course, always the knowledge that within two or three weeks (less in wartime) the job would have to be done again.

Left: Coaling ship aboard a British cruiser in 1914. Sack-barrows were

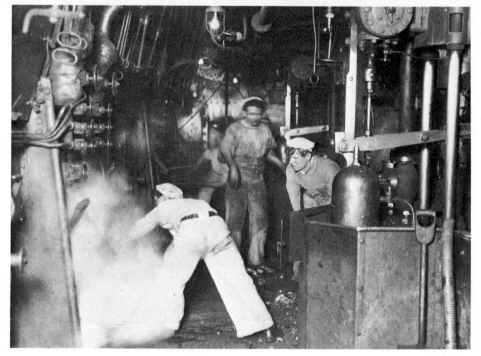

used to carry the coal to the team's particular chute down to the bunkers. Down below coal-trimmers worked in appalling conditions to stow the coal.
Top: Turkish prisoners fill coal bags in a collier.
Above: The end of it all: the stokehold in the battle-cruiser HMAS *Australia*. Although strength was a great asset to a stoker, he also had to learn skills which could mean making or losing a crucial extra knot.

Far left: A French sailor hangs out a shirt to dry amid recently scrubbed hammocks.

Top: Seamen repair a searchlight on board an American battleship during 1917. Note the lattice-mast peculiar to American-designed ships. It was believed to be less susceptible to serious damage in action. 'Stand-easy' has apparently just been piped, judging by the number of other men standing idly by.

Above: Blacksmiths at work on board the Italian battleship *San Marco* (1908) in 1918.

Left: A rating receives cordite charges from the magazine on board a German cruiser in September 1916, four months after the Battle of Jutland.

Left: Two Austrian sailors demonstrate the wearing of different types of breathing apparatus on board the armoured cruiser *Sankt Georg* (1903).

Above: Norwegian sailors pose in a photographer's studio-setting typical of the period, c1917.

Right: Officers of the cruiser *Vindictive*, which led the raid on Zeebrugge on 24 April 1918. Left to right, these are Surgeon Clegg, Commander Osborne, Captain Carpenter, Staff Surgeon McCutcheon, Paymaster Young, Gunner Cobby.

Right: Officers of the Royal Danish Navy entertain guests on the cramped quarterdeck of the torpedo boat *Soulven* (1911). The *Soulven,* 181 tons, had a top speed of 28.2 knots, and was armed with five 18-inch (457mm) torpedo tubes and two 12-pdr guns, one of which can be seen.

Below: Officers in the wardroom of the battle-cruiser HMAS *Australia.* On the extreme left, looking at the magazine, is a paymaster lieutenant, with next to him a lieutenant RNVR. On his left sits the chaplain. The commander in the centre of the picture is lighting his cigarette from the oil lamp hanging from the deck-head.

Bottom: Aboard the *San Marco* (1908), a pre-dreadnought battleship, Italian sailors write letters on a Sunday afternoon in September 1918. They are sheltered from the Mediterranean sun by a canvas awning.

Although the idea of seizing the Dardanelles in order to reduce the Turkish threat to Russia was sound enough, in the execution it failed totally, chiefly because of poor planning, and a complete absence of co-ordination between the Allied land and naval forces. The original plan was that the navy should force the passage alone, although even if it had been successful it is difficult to see how any advantage could have been consolidated without control of the shores. The stumbling block was the extensive Turkish minefield, which was covered by shore batteries equipped with searchlights. Minesweepers could not operate successfully because of the covering artillery, but until the

minefield was cleared the big ships could not get close enough for the accuracy required to silence well-sited field guns. The navy then withdrew until the troops arrived. When the ships had first begun the bombardment the defending troops were few in number. By the time the landings were made, reinforcements were in place and the footholds gained were costly in both life and material. The naval forces were British and French, and the soldiers were from Australia, New Zealand, France and Britain.

Above left: Relaxation for three British midshipmen on the island of Imbros.

Above: French sailors from the elderly battleship *Caudan* (1888) celebrate a success against a Turkish battery.

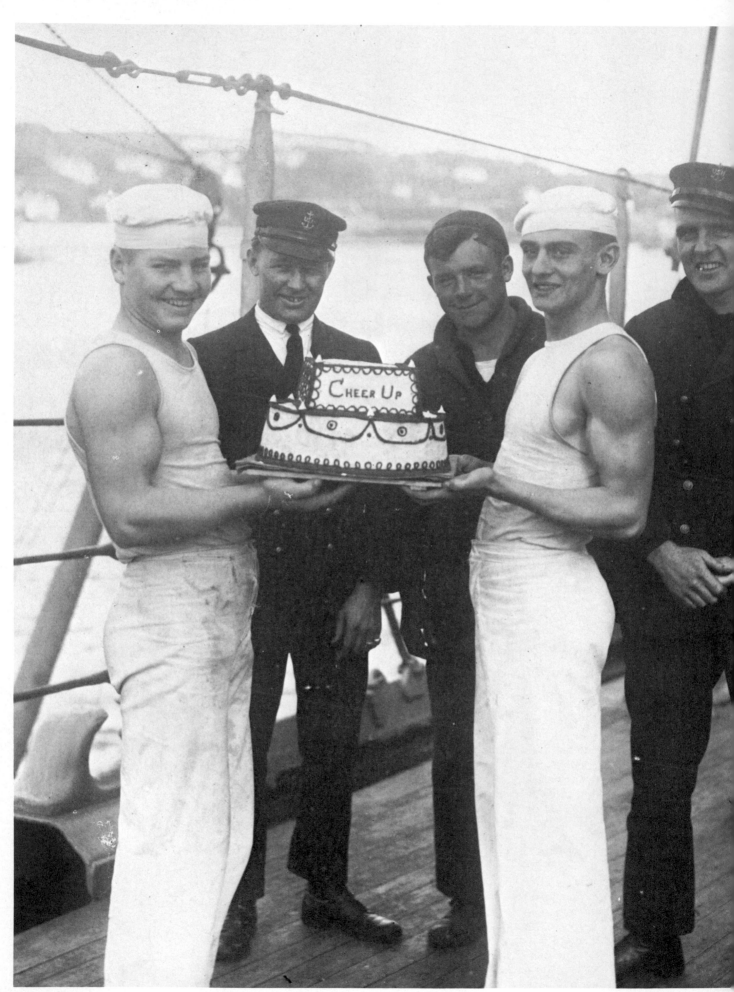

Left: Cooks aboard the depot ship
USS *Melville* hold an exhortatory
birthday cake for Admiral William S.
Sims, United States Navy.
Top: Two American sailors spend a
few moments making a fuss of 'Fritz',
the mascot aboard the USS *Melville*.
Above: An officer of the battle-cruiser
HMAS *Australia* takes the opportunity
of exercising the ship's pets on the
deserted deck. The circular steel plate
in the foreground is the hatch of a coal
chute leading to a bunker below.

Following the Armistice of 11 November 1918 the warships of the German navy were escorted to Britain to be placed under the watchful eye of the Royal Navy. The U-boats, which had to be surrendered immediately, were directed to Harwich, whence their crews were repatriated. The High Seas Fleet, which included nine battleships, five battle-cruisers, seven cruisers and fifty destroyers, was escorted to the huge anchorage at Scapa Flow in the Orkney Islands to be interned there, the ships remaining in the hands of German skeleton crews, until the peace conference decided what was to be done with them. Confined to their ships, the armaments and radios of which had all been immobilised, Rear-Admiral Reuter and his German crews were kept in complete ignorance as to what was occurring in the outside world. Acting on a 'suggestion' from the new socialist government in Germany that the ships should not be absorbed into the navies of the Allies, or sold by them for profit, Admiral Reuter secretly planned to scuttle his ships at the most opportune moment. His chance came on 21 June 1919, just a week before the peace treaty was signed, when the 1st Battle Squadron of the Royal Navy, then at Scapa Flow, put to sea on an exercise. At 1120 the order was given. Seacocks were opened and either their keys thrown into the sea or the valves damaged beyond all repair so that they could never be closed again. Of the battleships only the *Baden* was saved, after being beached by prompt action from naval vessels in the harbour. Similarly saved were three cruisers and nineteen destroyers, most of which could not see Admiral Reuter's signal because of an intervening headland. On the British side, the scuttling was looked upon as an act of treachery, a breach of faith for the German warships had been interned with their own crews on board and not, technically, surrendered. Germany, of course received the news with triumph and a salving of pride which lessened the humiliation of defeat.

Left, top: The crews of the scuttled German High Seas Fleet are welcomed as heroes by naval officers and civilian crowds on their return to Bremerhaven in the *Lisboa* in 1919.
Left, bottom: Members of a U-boat's crew with their belongings wait to be picked up after surrendering the submarine at the port of Harwich.
Right: The relative positions of the ensigns tell the story at Harwich in 1918.

CHAPTER 3
1919-1939

Disarmament cast a long shadow over the greatest part of the period between the wars because of the terms of the Washington Conference (1921-22) and the London Conference (1930). The Washington Naval Armaments Treaty was signed by Great Britain and her Dominions, the United States of America, Japan, France and Italy. Its provisions were to last for ten years, limiting the size and armament of capital ships (battleships and battle-cruisers), aircraft-carriers and cruisers, with capital ships and aircraft-carriers also limited by age and total tonnage allocations.

The London Treaty of 1930 renewed the terms of 1922 and fixed age limits and total tonnages for cruisers, which were divided into two classes according to the size of their main armament. Destroyers and submarines were also limited by age and total tonnage.

Between 1918 and 1939, warships and naval weapons change little. The one new type of warship to evolve was the aircraft-carrier.

The British navy had converted ships for use as seaplane carriers during the war and in 1918 the

Above: **Norwegian sailors in their hammocks aboard the coast defence battleship *Harald Haarfagre* (1897) in 1936.**

Left: **Refugees are landed at Marseilles from the destroyer HMS *Ardent* (1929) during the Spanish Civil War.**

Furious, originally designed as a battle-cruiser, was completed as an aircraft-carrier. She was at first fitted with a flying-off deck forward and after trials in July 1917, Squadron Commander Dunning made the first successful deck landing. As a result of this experience, a longer, landing-on deck was added aft of the superstructure, and the *Furious* was completed in this form in 1918. It was then realised that the funnels and bridge formed too much of a hazard and that they would either have to be removed entirely or re-sited to one side of a continuous flight-deck, in either case a revolutionary idea in design.

The first 'flat-top' carriers appeared in the 1920s in the navies of Britain, the United States, France and Japan. Several of these were converted from designs for capital ships which could not meet the terms of the Washington Conference Naval Limitation Treaty.

In the *Lexington* and *Saratoga,* completed respectively in 1927 and 1928, the United States had the largest carriers afloat until the beginning of the Second World War. Of the other naval powers, neither Italy nor Germany completed any aircraft-carriers.

Few battleships were built in the years of peace until after Japan had unilaterally abrogated the limitation treaties in 1936. Even then Great Britain, the United States and France became involved with new restrictive agreements with Germany and Russia.

While they lasted, the limitation treaties had a

marked influence on battleship design, noticeable in Britain's *Nelson* and *Rodney,* and later the French battle-cruisers *Dunkerque* and *Strasbourg.* In all these ships the entire main armament was forward of the midships superstructure, an arrangement which had the advantage of allowing the armour to be concentrated and the best use to be made of the limited tonnage permitted. Britain did not repeat the experiment, though France did with the *Richelieu* class. France was the first power to use the quadruple gun turret, an arrangement used by Great Britain in the *King George V* class battleships, but not repeated in the *Vanguard,* Britain's last battleship.

Battleship construction by the United States was limited to the three *Maryland* class vessels built during the early 1920s. As long as the treaties were upheld, the agreed ratio of the Washington Conference permitted only two capital ships for Japan and one for Italy, although two ships of the *Littorio* class were completed during the arms race in the last years of the 1930s.

The numerous types of cruiser built in the years before the First World War were reduced by the treaties to two: light cruisers with guns up to and including 6-inch (152.4mm), and heavy cruisers carrying larger guns. Cruisers were given a greater striking power by an increase in the number of guns carried, for whereas the largest number of guns carried in the main armament of a cruiser during the First World War had been seven, between the wars so-called light cruisers were built to carry fifteen 6-inch guns, and heavy cruisers carried up to ten 8-inch (203mm) guns. By the treaty limitations, any warship over 10,000 tons was classed as a capital ship and had to be included in the allocation of tonnage for that class. Warships smaller than cruisers were subject only to total tonnage limits. Destroyers increased in size and armament, the largest being the French *Mogador* class of the early 1930s with a displacement of nearly 3,000 tons and carrying eight 5.5-inch (139.7mm) guns. Submarines also increased in size and their torpedo armament was enlarged, but the technical advances during peacetime were limited. Their engines were quieter, however, and with more efficient batteries they could remain submerged longer than had been possible during the First World War. The considerable improvement in the technical development of radio also afforded increased tactical mobility.

Because of its importance later, the subject of German naval rearmament is considered separately.

The Treaty of Versailles had left the Weimar Republic with a navy consisting of a few pre-dreadnought battleships, six light cruisers and a dozen destroyers—a return in fact to the coast defence navy of the 1880s. With quite separate and specific limits placed on its navy, the Weimar Republic was not invited to send representatives either to Washington in

1921 or to London in 1930.

In 1928 the oldest of the battleships allowed to Germany became due for replacement. Although to all intents and purposes the new ship fulfilled the requirements of the Treaty of Versailles, which limited any replacement to a maximum 10,000 tons, the *Deutschland* was nearer 12,000 tons, a well-kept secret for some years. The new warship caused a sensation when launched in 1931, to be completed the following year. Designed as a commerce-raider, the *Deutschland* was lightly armoured but carried a greater broadside than any warship faster than herself, with the exception of the three British battle-cruisers. Her advent, and the announcement that two similar ships were to follow, caused the French to produce the *Strasbourg* and *Dunkerque* as a counter.

The Anglo-German Naval Treaty of 1935, offered by Britain after Hitler had formally renounced the limitations of the Treaty of Versailles, allowed Germany five battleships, five heavy cruisers, eleven light cruisers and sixty-four destroyers, with a submarine fleet rather less than half that of Britain. When war was declared the German fleet consisted of the battle-cruisers (or small battleships) *Scharnhorst* and *Gneisenau,* the three *Deutschland* class ships (known in Britain as 'pocket-battleships'), two heavy cruisers, six light cruisers, thirty-four destroyers and fifty-seven submarines. In addition the battleships *Bismarck* and *Tirpitz* and another heavy cruiser were under construction. Even with the latter completed, this fleet would be no more than a quarter of the strength envisaged by the strategic Z-Plan, devised in 1938, which presupposed that conflict with Great Britain could be avoided until at least 1944.

The other countries with naval forces of any size, but who were scarcely major powers at sea, contented themselves with the addition to their fleet of cruisers, destroyers, submarines and patrol craft.

Not surprisingly, training and 'goodwill cruises' formed the largest part of any navy's activities in peacetime. Navies were often able to render early assistance in the event of natural disaster such as an earthquake or volcanic eruption. This sort of naval operation is typified in the photograph of the German pre-dreadnought *Elsass,* shown icebound during her mission to aid the crews of two merchant ships caught in the ice. Occasionally the disaster was manmade: a photograph shows the British destroyer *Ardent* at Marseilles landing forlorn refugees from the Spanish Civil War.

But in all the training, all the exercises, no one foresaw that the age-old concept of war at sea—a duel between big ships with big guns—was all but dead. The key to predominance at sea lay in the skies above it; and the aircraft-carrier was very soon to become the new capital ship.

Top: The British battleship *Rodney*, with a stern that appears truncated, had a main armament of nine 16-inch (456mm) guns in three triple turrets forward of the bridge.

Above: The British heavy cruiser *Sussex* seems very unstreamlined compared with other nations' heavy cruisers, and had a main armament of eight 8-inch (203mm) guns.

An informal part of the celebrations
arranged for the Peace Day holiday in
July 1919.

Left, above: A children's party in progress on board the battle-cruiser HMS *Repulse* (1916), while at Cape Town during her 1924 world tour. Every available flag has been used as decorative bunting. With the emergency capstan bars in place for use as seats, the steam-driven capstan on the fo'c's'le has become a merry-go-round. Because of the heat, a canvas awning has been rigged over the foremost (A) turret. The sailor in the foreground is standing between the anchor cables for which the capstan was normally used.

Left, below: French signalmen extract flags from the signal lockers on board the light cruiser *Duguay-Trouin* during manoeuvres off Quiberon on 25 October 1934. The *Duguay-Trouin* was the flagship of Vice-Admiral Darlan, in command of the 2nd Cruiser Squadron and later a key political figure in the Second World War.

Right: An American signalman communicates with a light cruiser of the *Omaha* class by semaphore. Made obsolescent with the use of morse code by radio or focussing signal lamp, practice in semaphore was still considered useful since radio silence might be essential and the lamps out of action as a result of battle damage.

Left: French sailors of the destroyer *Fougueux* relax; inevitably, someone on board plays the accordion.

Top: Aboard the French training cruiser *Jeanne d'Arc* (1930) the gun crew of a 3-inch (75mm) anti-aircraft gun relax after an exercise. Note the size of the anchor stowed nearby.

Above: Since the later years of the nineteenth century there has been a strong tradition of foreign navies purchasing warships built in Britain. In 1912 Greece bought from Argentina four destroyers ordered from Cammell Laird Ltd. Renamed, they served in the Greek navy and were brought back to Cowes, Isle of Wight, in 1924 for a major refit by J. S. White & Co Ltd. The photograph shows Greek sailors standing by during the refit, grouped round the midships 4-inch (102mm) gun on board the *Leon* (1911).

Left: Kit inspection on board an American flagship. In the cramped quarters on board a warship it is important that both the ship and the men are kept clean and tidy. Regular kit inspections are therefore necessary to check for kit deficiencies or neglect, because an improperly clothed or ill-equipped man may breed disease or be unable to carry out his duty. Nor is the identical layout required merely a matter of smartness and discipline: a standard pattern in the layout enables both sailor and inspecting officer to check every item without wasting time.

Top: Pay day aboard the battleship HMS *Rodney* (1925) in 1930. Pay is still issued in a similar manner today following a pattern long established by the time of the earlier pay day photograph in 1895 (see page 40). Aboard the *Rodney*, payment is made by the Paymaster Lieutenant-Commander, who now (following the end of the First World War)) wears the curl above his stripes, which are separated by white bands.
Above: Representatives of each seamen's mess line up to collect the rum ration in a 'fanny' during 1933.

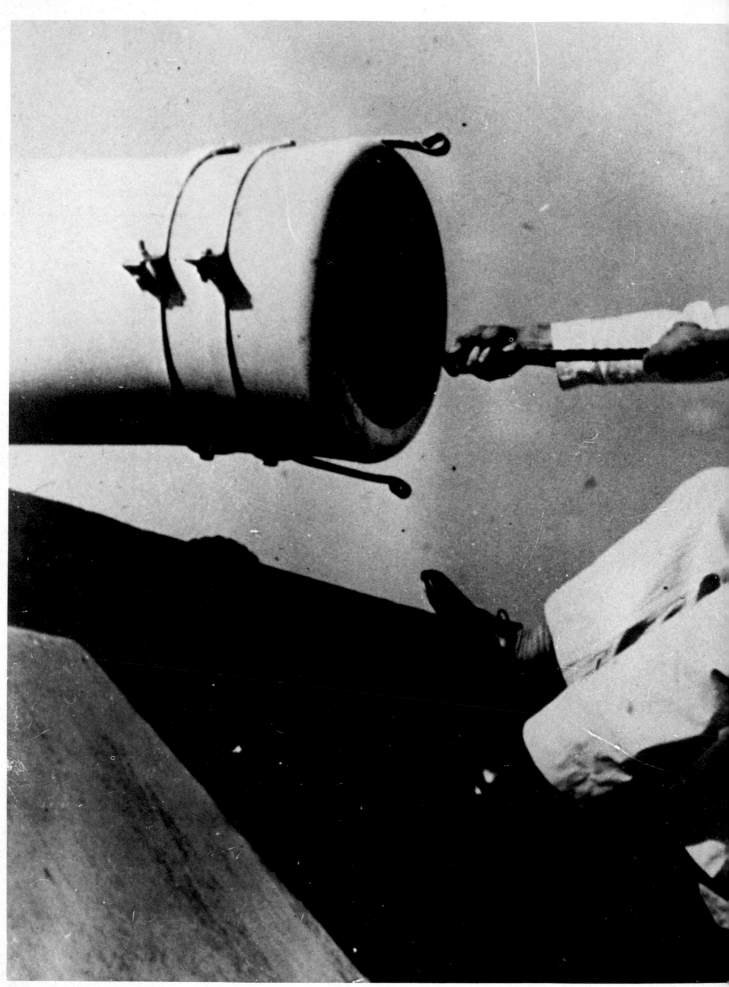

Previous page: American sailors clean the barrel of a 14-inch (355.6-mm) gun on board a battleship.

Left: Japanese marines on board the cruiser *Ashigara* (1928). Since it was clearly advantageous to have as part of the complement of a large warship a body of men especially trained in land warfare without involving skilled seamen, most maritime nations developed a Marine Corps. On board their roles include acting as sentries, ammunition numbers, gun crews and bandsmen.

Below: Danish marines with their arms stacked. The length of the sword-bayonet proved to be an unnecessary encumbrance, difficult to use. By 1939 most countries had changed to the short, but equally effective and handier bayonet 9-12 inches (23-30 cm) long. It is worth noting, however, that only a small proportion of battle casualties were caused by the bayonet.

Right, above: Dutch seamen carry cartridge cases for 5.9-inch (150mm) guns. The bags over the gun muzzles are to protect the polished inner surface of the barrels from rust.

Right, below: Part of a 6-inch (152.4mm) gun crew during a practice firing aboard HMS *Iron Duke*. The *Iron Duke* was Admiral Jellicoe's flagship at Jutland, but was demilitarised under the terms of the Treaty of London in 1931-1932. She was rearmed as a gunnery training ship just before the Second World War. In the Royal Navy the main armament turrets were given letters starting from the bows: 'A', 'B', 'X' and 'Y'. If there were five turrets, the centre one was 'Q'. In major vessels marines usually manned X turret and seamen the remainder. When guns' crews were 'closed up' in a capital ship, more than 500 men took up their action stations.

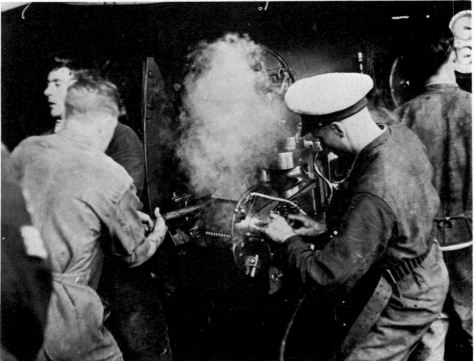

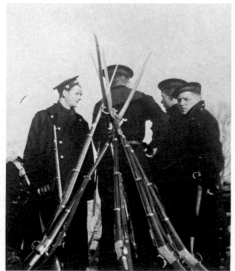

Left: Even a landlocked country like Czechoslovakia has the need for a certain amount of naval expertise on the Elbe and the Vltava. In the photograph marines adjust the helmet of a diver on board a patrol boat.

Top: The training of officers is an important item in creating and keeping an efficient service. All navies of any size have established colleges where young men receive not only the specialised training appropriate to their calling but, in addition, a good general education. Young Americans can be trained at the Naval Academy at Annapolis, Maryland, and in the 1930s the future officers of the German Navy went to school at Ploen in northern Germany. Prospective officers in the Royal Navy receive their initial training at the *Britannia* Royal Naval College, Dartmouth. Part of their training is done at sea for short periods on board small craft such as minesweepers. The photograph shows a navigation class practising the use of the sextant on board the minesweeper HMS *Carstairs*.

Above right: An adequately trained reserve force is also important to a navy. The Royal Navy has three types of reservist: when regular service men retire they become part of the Royal Fleet Reserve for a number of years; professional sailors in the merchant service can join the Royal Naval Reserve; amateur sailors, or those who wish to be, join the Royal Naval Volunteer Reserve. The photograph shows men of the RNVR at gun drill aboard the light cruiser HMS *Curacoa* (1917) during a summer training cruise. The petty officer in charge is a Gunner's Mate.

Above: The USS *Saratoga* (1925) in 1934. With her sistership *Lexington,* one of the first aircraft-carriers in the US fleet, the *Saratoga* had a splendid record during the Second World War. She is seen here with almost all of her complement of combat aircraft on the flight-deck.

Left: A German destroyer of the *Beitzen* class (1935-37) on an exercise in the Baltic Sea, August 1939. The destroyer has fired a practice torpedo which is being spotted by the seaplane.

Right: The *Foch,* a *Dupleix* class (1927-30) cruiser of the French navy, about to launch an aircraft by catapult. These ships came very close to the cruiser limits laid down at the Washington Conference in 1921-22. Their armament consisted of eight 8-inch (203mm) guns plus eight heavy and eight light anti-aircraft guns. The huge 'arms' on either side of the after funnel are the cranes for recovering seaplanes from the water after reconnaissance or spotting flights.

Overleaf: The German training ship *Elsass* (1903) on a rescue mission in the mid-1920s. Two merchant ships had been caught in the ice and the *Elsass,* herself now temporarily icebound, has just 'landed' sledges to take food and medical supplies across the ice to the trapped merchant seamen.

Left: On 16 March 1930 the Chilean submarine depot-ship *Araucano* was formally handed over by the builders, Messrs Vickers Ltd, at Barrow-in-Furness shipyard. Members of the crew cheer as the flag of Chile is raised at the ensign staff.

Top: After five years as Commander-in-Chief of the British Mediterranean Fleet, Admiral Sir William Fisher bids farewell to his command. Admiral Fisher was one who inspired great loyalty and affection and the fleet made much of his departure. After a farewell dinner aboard the battle-cruiser *Renown,* he was rowed back to his flagship the *Queen Elizabeth* by his subordinate admirals, escorted by an oared cutter manned by captains. As the *Queen Elizabeth* steamed slowly out of the harbour at Alexandria the next morning, he was cheered to the echo by each ship she passed. The photograph was taken from the bridge of the cruiser *Sussex,* and the tall figure of Fisher can just be seen standing alone on the flagship's B turret.

Above: The 'pocket-battleship' *Deutschland* arriving at Wilhelmshaven on 16 June 1937 bearing the bodies of thirty-one German volunteers killed in the Spanish Civil War.

Above: Between the wars it was the practice in some ships to weigh the members of the ship's company at the beginning and at the end of the commission. The photograph shows a young sailor being weighed by a Physical Training Instructor on board the cruiser HMS *London* (1927) at the start of a new commission. A Petty Officer gunlayer acts as recorder, and the Divisional Lieutenant looks on.

Right: A capstan worked by manpower has been a rarity on a warship only since the end of the nineteenth century. It is seen here, however, on board the cruiser HMS *Devonshire,* sister ship to the *London,* at Alexandria in 1936, during 'General Drill'. Periods of 'General Drill' were used by captains to test the efficiency and ingenuity of their ship's company, for the orders issued were often unusual and unexpected. The black armbands worn by the officers indicate that the incident occurred during the period of mourning after George V's death.

Left, above: The Swedish *Gotland* was an interesting 'small navy' variation on the standard aircraft-carrier. Termed an 'aircraft cruiser', she displaced only 5,200 tons and had no flight-deck suitable for landing on, but merely a large parking deck aft. She carried eight seaplanes which were launched by catapult and hoisted inboard from the sea on their return. The disadvantage inherent in this method was the near impossibility of launching and certainly of recovering aircraft in bad weather. Before the advent of radar, spotter aircraft were carried on many larger warships to provide long-range reconnaissance or to spot the fall of shot and radio back corrections to the firing ship.

Left, below: Dutch sailors on board a small warship at the universal chore, in western navies, of peeling potatoes. The job may have been tedious, but there were worse thingsto do than sit in the sunshine in convivial company, gossiping, and on this occasion at least, able to smoke.

Right, above: Peeling potatoes for the 1,323 officers and men of the battleship USS *New Mexico* (1917) would have been a completely uneconomic use of manpower. The picture, taken in 1919, shows the electric potato peeler fitted in the spacious galley, of which only a part can be seen. The United States Navy was the first to introduce many of these labour-saving devices on board warships.

Right, below: On a cruise in September 1936 cadets from the *Britannia* Royal Navy College at Dartmouth patronise the canteen during a 'stand-easy'. The stripe on the sleeve of the tall cadet indicates that he is a cadet-captain.

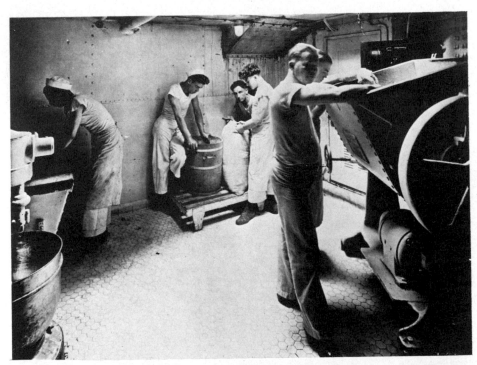

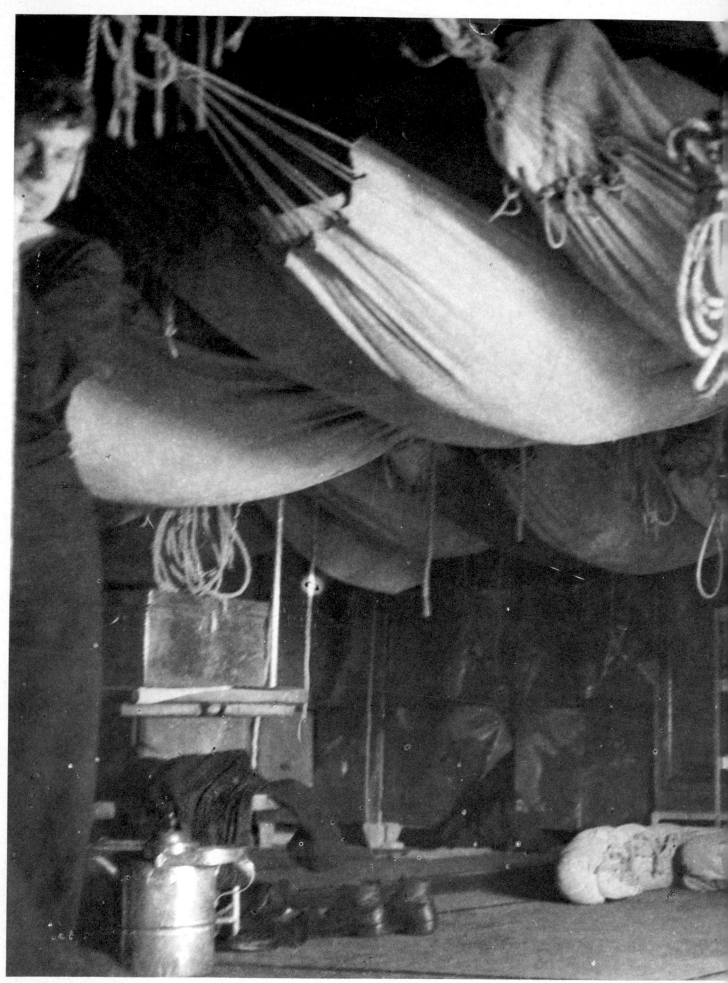

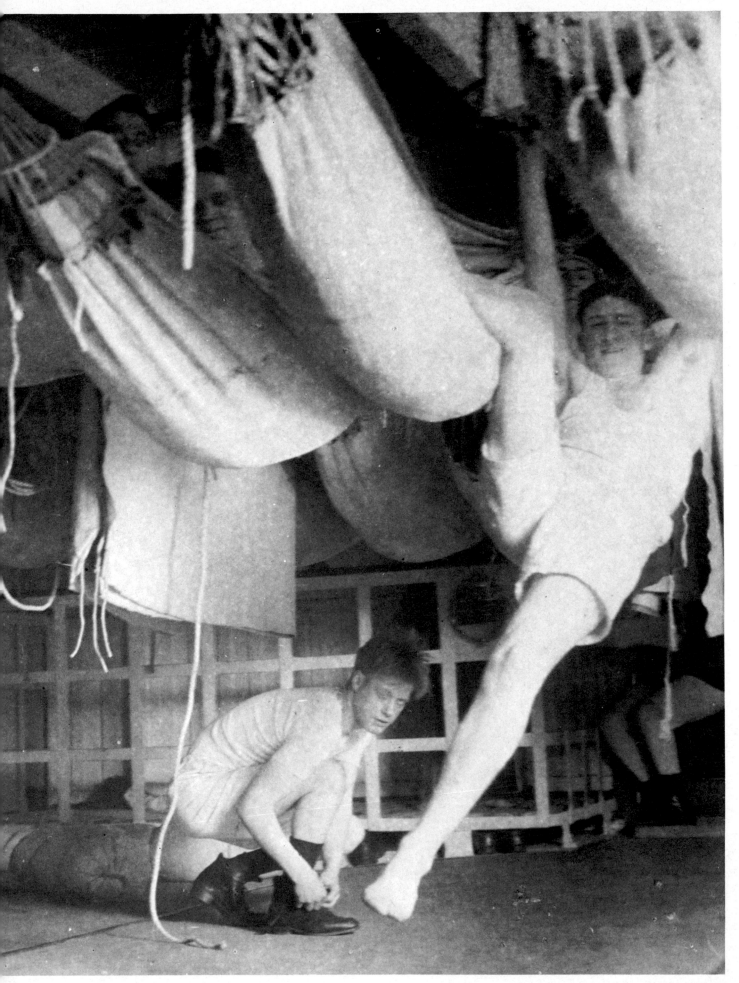

Previous page: 'Wakey, wakey! Come along then, rise and shine the sun's scorchin' your bleedin' eyes out!' So went the patter of the duty petty officer as he roused the messdecks at 0545. The cry of 'show a leg!' lasted until the middle years of the twentieth century too. 'Show a leg' as an order connected with waking sailors dates from the eighteenth century when, while ships were in harbour, the womenfolk of the crew were allowed to sleep on board. The order 'show a leg!' was to enable the boatswain's mates of the day to distinguish between male and female occupants of a cot or hammock; women were allowed to lie-in for an extra hour. Notice the boots, for with the First World War the habit of going barefoot passed. Parts of the upper deck, especially the quarterdeck, were still planked in teak over the armour plating, but all lower decks were of steel, and cold to the touch in the early morning. 'Lash-up and stow!' was another early morning cry, ordering that with the bedding laid inside, the hammocks should be secured with their lashings and stowed.

Left: Throughout the navy washing is known as 'dhobeying', a corruption of Hindustani as in 'dhobi-walla' or washerman, dating from the days of the Naval Brigade in India during the Mutiny in 1857. These boy seamen at HMS *Ganges,* the naval training establishment at Shotley near Harwich, are doing their dhobeying in the old-fashioned way: on the wash-house floor, or deck, with soap, water and lots of scrubbing.

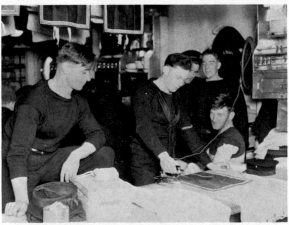

Right, top: In the sailmaker's shop on board the battle-cruiser HMS *Renown* (1916) in the North Sea in 1932, they are making black canvas searchlight covers. The third man has slipped in for a chat or perhaps to persuade the petty officer sailmaker to make him some small 'rabbit', an item for personal use illegally made from government material in the navy's valuable time.

Right, centre: A domestic scene on the mess-deck of an aircraft-carrier. Note the creases, as prescribed by regulations, in the collars hanging on the hammock rails. On the table is a ditty-box, the lockable scrubbed wooden box in which a man could keep his valuables.

Right, bottom: A sailmaker at work on an awning. On his left sleeve are the crown and crossed anchors of his rank as petty officer. On his right sleeve is the star above the crossed needles denoting his trade as sailmaker.

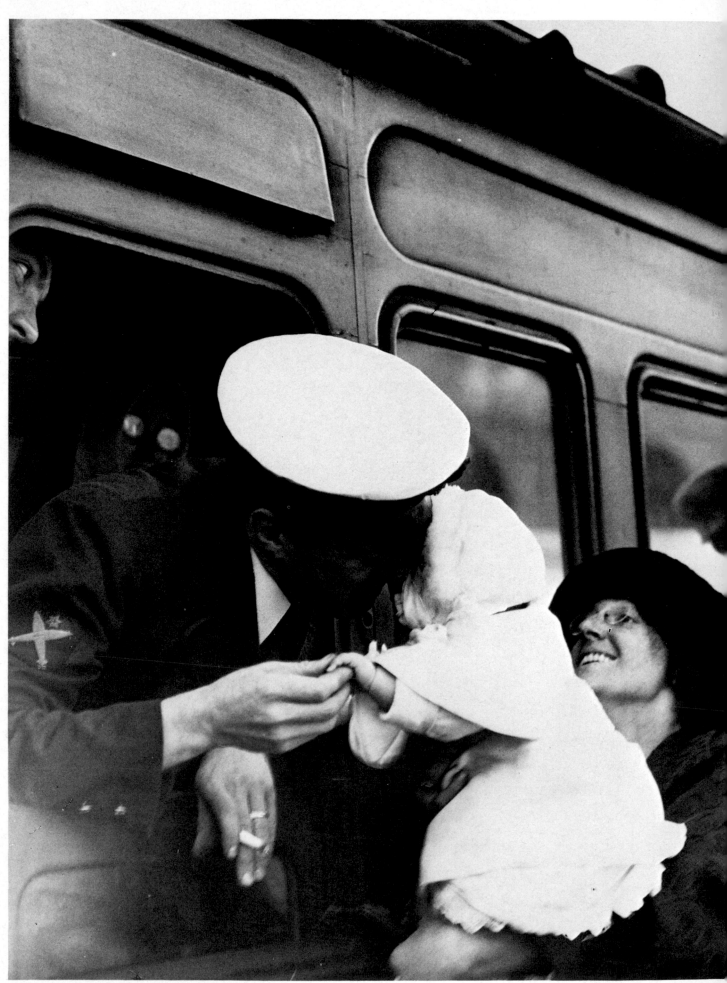

Left: A petty officer torpedo gunner says goodbye to his daughter on returning from leave in August 1923.
Above: Leave has to be arranged so that the ship is manned at all times, which is not normally difficult except at Christmas. The usual procedure is that the majority who want Christmas leave go early enough to return on about 28 December. This allows the skeleton crew left on board to have leave over the New Year. There is usually a sufficiently large number of Scots in any ship's company to make the arrangement acceptable to all. The photograph shows some of the first party leaving HMS *Southampton* (1936) at Chatham Dockyard on 14 December 1937. The majority of the sailors are carrying the small suitcase recently introduced to replace the wooden ditty-box. The black searchlight covers similar to that being made in the picture on page 101 can be seen on the searchlight platforms. The starboard triple torpedo-tubes are visible below the after funnel.

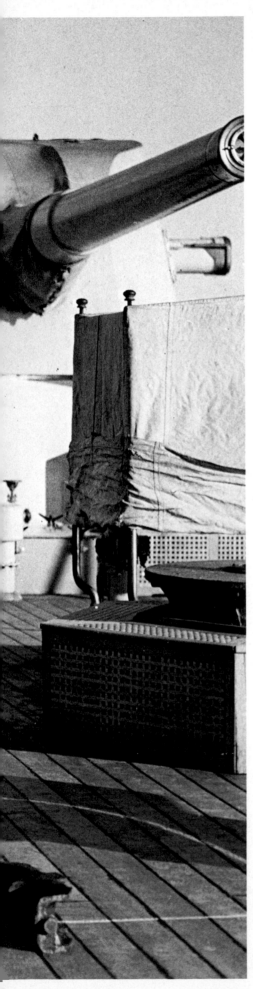

Left: Sport, particularly in the form of team games, is encouraged in every navy, not merely because it provides a generally pleasant way of keeping fit, but also because it fosters team spirit and an *esprit de corps* that may be invaluable during the most difficult moments in action. Within the ship mess-deck plays mess-deck and watch plays watch. The ship will enter the fleet tournament or play a local civilian team when in port. Best of all are the games against the 'chummy-ship', old friends and rivals on the squadron or station. Field sports usually need facilities ashore, provided in abundance at most naval bases. Rowing (in the navy usually in whalers, gigs or cutters) is an obvious sport. A few others, such as boxing and fencing, are also suitable for the more cramped conditions on board, while others can be adapted to the peculiar conditions and confined space of a deck. Deck hockey, with a rope ring for the ball, and no rules to speak of, is one of the latter games. The picture shows an evening game in progress on the quarterdeck of the cruiser HMS *London* (1927), the teams being from the officers of the Wardroom and the junior sub-lieutenants and midshipmen of the Gun Room, with the latter about to score. There were, no doubt, drinks on the result.

Right, above: Boxing is popular in the Royal Navy, but it is strictly controlled with no contest allowed longer than three 3-minute rounds. Frequently the rounds are shorter. The photograph shows boxing, although clearly not a serious competition bout, two fencers and two who have been bayonet fighting. All are midshipmen.

Right, below: A different method of taking exercise. The ship's company of the battle-cruiser HMS *Renown* (1916) 'warm up' on the fo'c's'le in the brisk morning air of November in the North Sea, while the Royal Marine band provides the music. From the look of the deck in the foreground (compare it with the deck in the other pictures on this page) the First Lieutenant will find yet another means of exercise for some luckless sailors later on in the day. Tompions bearing the ship's badge keep the weather out of the polished barrels on the 15-inch (381mm) guns; above them are the range-finders. In the days before radar, range-finding had to be managed with optical instruments with as great a base measurement as possible, working on either the stereoscopic or the coincidence principle.

Left: The island of Mudros had little to offer sailors for the 'run ashore', but they frequently went inland for a few hours just to get away from the navy. This party seems to have had a good afternoon. The smarly dressed petty officer obviously considers himself the leader of the group, and has a way with children and animals. The sailor holding the little boy's hand is prepared to call it a day, whilst on the extreme right, the sun, combined perhaps with rum no doubt illegally saved and illegally brought ashore, has had its effect.

Top: Sailors and marines, mostly from HMS *Repulse* (1916), with visitors on the fo'c's'le of the battle-cruiser during the Portsmouth Navy Week in August 1928. In the background can be seen the distinctive flight deck of the aircraft-carrier HMS *Furious* (1917).

Above: An American petty officer and rating sightseeing in China during a goodwill visit in the 1920s.

Overleaf: The visit of Queen Wilhelmina of the Netherlands and Princess Juliana to the Royal Netherlands Navy, on board the cruiser *Java* on the occasion of the ship's commissioning ceremony in May 1925.

CHAPTER 4

1939-1945

The problems facing the British navy in 1939 were very much those it had faced in 1914. As before, it was the major naval force facing the Germans. The problems were, however, to become infinitely harder. Close blockade was out of the question, and so with the Channel secured by mines, submarines and air cover, the Home Fleet, as the main striking force of the British navy was now called, retired once more to Scapa Flow. It was difficult enough, during the long hours of darkness and bad weather that accompanied the winter months, to prevent units of the German navy reaching the open waters of the North Atlantic, even when they were based on German ports. By midsummer 1940, the whole of Norway was in German hands and the gap through which raiders might pass had increased from about 300 miles (480km) to roughly twice that, with a further 200 miles (320km), the Denmark Strait, between Iceland and Greenland. To a certain extent the difficulties had been reduced somewhat by the

Left: **A scene that typifies the horror of war at sea : an American tanker, torpedoed off the eastern coast of the USA in 1942, is a raging inferno.**
Above: **A wounded pilot, having landed his aircraft safely on the flight deck, is lifted clear. A member of his crew looks on anxiously.**

British occupation of Iceland in May 1940 in order to deny to Germany what would have been an invaluable outpost. All the same, the task then confronting the British navy was enormous.

To make matters worse, after the fall of France, Germany was able to take full advantage of the whole of the French coastline on the Atlantic Ocean. Not only was this especially important in the submarine war, as will be seen, but it also meant that surface raiders harassed in the Atlantic could find shelter and repair facilities in the former French naval bases of Brest and St Nazaire.

German raiders, supported by a well organised system for replenishment by tankers and other supply ships, had been sent out in August 1939 against the possibility of war with Great Britain. Of these, the *Deutschland* achieved little, but the several armed merchant-ship raiders took a heavy toll of Allied shipping before they were finally caught. The most successful, and most famous, raider of all was the 'pocket battleship' *Graf Spee,* sistership to the *Deutschland.* Brought to action at last by the 8-inch (203mm) gun cruiser *Exeter* and two light cruisers, the *Graf Spee* almost disabled the former and also put out of action half the main 6-inch (152.4mm) armament of the *Ajax* before seeking shelter in the neutral Paraguayan port of Montevideo. Three days later, however, when the time came for her to sail, her captain chose to blow up his ship immediately outside the harbour rather than risk her being sunk in shallow water with perhaps too little explosives left on board to prevent the enemy from recovering secret equipment from the wreck.

The elimination of the commerce-raiders in distant waters proved to be far more difficult in the Second World War than in the First, and such raiders continued to be a menace until the end of 1942. The greatest threat from surface raiders lay in the North Atlantic, because of the German bases provided by the occupation of Norway and France.

The first such action occurred late in 1940, when the third 'pocket battleship', the *Admiral Scheer,* suddenly appeared before an eastbound convoy of thirty-eight ships. The only escort vessel of any force was the armed but unarmoured merchant cruiser *Jervis Bay,* equipped with old 6-inch guns. By steaming straight for her more powerful enemy she was able to delay the raider for nearly half an hour, by which time darkness was approaching and the *Admiral Scheer* succeeded in finding and sinking only five ships of the now scattered convoy.

The *Admiral Scheer* continued on a successful five-month cruise ranging as far afield as the Indian Ocean. The cruiser *Hipper* met with only moderate success in two shorter voyages, while the battle-cruisers *Scharnhorst* and the *Gneisenau* operating together in February and March 1941 sank twenty-two ships, a modest enough return for the force employed over a period of six weeks.

The appearance of the *Admiral Scheer* in the North Atlantic in the previous November had led to the strengthening of convoy escorts, a move which greatly limited the effectiveness of the German ships. It was no part of the raider's job to risk serious damage in any unnecessary brush with major warships.

The final action of this phase of the German blockade came in May 1941 when the new German battleship *Bismarck,* which had sailed on 18 May in company with the heavy cruiser *Prinz Eugen,* was finally sunk about 400 miles (640km) west of the French port of Brest. The *Bismarck,* built with the many compartmental subdivisions which had made the German capital ships so difficult to sink at Jutland, and for the same reasons, proved equally hard to despatch. Further, in the early minutes of an intermittent running fight that lasted three days, she sank the battle-cruiser *Hood,* the biggest ship in the British navy.

The remainder of the sorties made by German surface vessels were not in the Atlantic but in the icy waters to the north of Norway, on the convoy route to Murmansk in northern Russia. Early in 1942, Hitler became obsessed with the idea that Allied forces would invade Norway, and as a result the main components of the German navy, other than submarines, were concentrated in Norwegian waters. At the same time, they were conveniently placed to interfere with the convoys whose cargoes had played a significant part in frustrating the German attempt to put Russia out of the war in one swift, demoralising campaign.

The *Tirpitz,* sistership to the *Bismarck,* was now ready, but on her first sortie she missed the convoy that was her prey, and on her second she was withdrawn on Hitler's orders until the aircraft-carrier of the British intercepting force had been put out of action. Except as a potential raider, the *Tirpitz* contributed nothing to the German effort thereafter, for having suffered severe damage in an attack by British midget submarines, she became a constant target for British bombers and was eventually sunk in Tromso fjord in November 1944. Raids by the *Hipper* and the *Lützow* (the *Deutschland* renamed) had been unsuccessful and the last attempt by surface vessels to plunder the Arctic convoys resulted in the *Scharnhorst* being overwhelmed and sunk by the battleship *Duke of York* in December 1943.

Meanwhile, following the loss of the *Bismarck* in May 1941, Hitler had turned to an all-out effort by the U-boats in the Battle of the Atlantic.

The fall of France had made a vast difference in the capabilities of Admiral Dönitz's U-boat fleet. Submarines no longer had to make the long and hazardous passage northabout round Scotland to reach home, for now they were based on the coast of western France, notably at Brest and Lorient. They operated in packs of five or six, controlled by radio from France with long-range aircraft spotting for them. They no longer attacked submerged, in which condition their slow speed demanded exact positioning for an effective attack and left them vulnerable to reaction from escort vessels. Instead they attacked by night and on the surface, for then their speed of 16 knots was twice that of the average convoy and their low profile made them very difficult to spot.

Nevertheless, by the end of 1941 the formation of escort groups, the provision of constant aircraft escorts operating from the new escort carriers, the use of long-range aircraft from land bases, and above all perhaps, the wider use of radar, resulted in the U-boat offensive being contained. It is also true that some U-boats had been transferred to the Mediterranean and to the Arctic, but the lot of those in the Atlantic was becoming increasingly difficult.

Germany was to receive encouragement from an unexpected quarter, however. In the last months of 1941 Allied shipping losses had averaged 135,000 tons a month in all theatres; by June 1942 losses in the Western Atlantic alone had reached 500,000 tons a month. The reason for this German success had been the entry into the war by the United States after

Japan's attack on her Pacific Fleet at Pearl Harbor. Just like her allies earlier in the war, the United States was slow in getting to grips with the realities of war, and for many months German submarines found easy pickings on the US east coast from the Caribbean to New England. The situation even provoked a smaller version of Lend-Lease, this time in reverse, for in May the British navy lent the United States ten corvettes and twenty-four trawlers. At that time only one U-boat had been sunk off the American coast. The United States ignored the lessons that Britain, too, had learned the hard way: coastal convoys were not introduced until May. With the almost complete introduction of convoys by the end of July, the German returns diminished so sharply that the submarines were called off the American coast, with the exception of a few long-range U-boats that continued to operate in the West Indies, refuelled by a new submarine tanker fresh from home.

Invigorated by its success, the German navy turned its U-boats once more to the central areas of the North Atlantic. There were about 140 operational submarines available at that time, backed up by an additional 120 working up in the safety of the Baltic. Submarines were being built at a rate of twenty to thirty each month, the peak figure of operational U-boats being in excess of 200 early in 1943.

Of the 140 submarines, twenty were harassing the Arctic convoys and a similar number was operating in the Mediterranean Sea. Roughly 100 were in the Atlantic, some of them working off the coast of South America and Africa. The remaining eighty or more concentrated on the convoys passing both ways between North America and Great Britain.

With the increased use of long-range aircraft, the U-boats had been forced to concentrate their attacks farther and farther westward. There was still, however, 'the black pit', a belt of ocean some 500 miles (800km) wide beyond the range of land-based aircraft. It was the presence of these radar-equipped aircraft that kept German submarines submerged and so at a disadvantage, but in 'the black pit' the wolfpacks were able to use their much greater speed on the surface, and to choose the moment to strike the convoy from several different directions at once.

Shipping losses were high (in November 1942 more then 700,000 tons), indeed the highest for the whole war. With a brief respite in December and January when bad weather reduced losses by about half, the number of sinkings rose rapidly again in the spring. But in early summer, although individual attacks were still pressed home with the utmost ferocity, the tonnage lost declined sharply. The battle had been won. The reason was that despite the heavy toll in shipping (and towards the end of 1942 the steady loss of merchant ship crews was also a worrying factor), the

U-boats were having to pay too high a price. In the first half of 1942, twenty-four U-boats had been sunk; in the second half of the year sixty-four had been sunk, in each case the majority of them in the North Atlantic. In February, March and April 1943, U-boat losses averaged eighteen a month, but in May they jumped to a staggering forty-one, almost a third of the total operational force. No navy could stand losses of that order, and Dönitz either sent the remainder south-west of the Azores or else called them home. The attacks on convoys were renewed later, but never again on the same scale or with anything approaching the same results.

The U-boat campaigns had been defeated by the use of more escort vessels, especially small carriers, and improved techniques; the use of long-range aircraft played a crucial part in the victory, but above all, the single most important weapon was radar, in its simple form at first and later in the device that enabled the hunter to 'see' the submarines at long range in fog, cloud or darkness.

This account has concentrated on the Battle of the Atlantic, but there was considerable U-boat activity in other theatres of war. No doubt German submariners would agree with British and American sailors that unpleasant as the North Atlantic undoubtedly was, for sheer hardship in just living, even without the rigours of action, the seas to the north of Norway in which the Arctic convoy battles were fought must take pride of place. Tactically the feature that distinguished these actions from those in the Atlantic was that except very locally and for the relatively short period when carrier-borne aircraft were present, the air belonged to Germany, so that there was no respite for those convoys at sea during the almost continuous daylight of the Arctic summer.

Paradoxically, the tactical conditions obtaining for the Arctic convoys were similar to those in the Mediterranean, where the climate, at least, was infinitely more bearable. In each case, however, the convoys were exposed to continuous air attack during the hours of daylight; and if the summer days were shorter in the Mediterranean, the weather was also better and hampered enemy air operations much less often. In each case too, there was always the possibility, too often the reality, of interference by powerful enemy surface forces.

British submarines in the Atlantic theatre had a different role to play from that of the U-boats. Except for the few weeks at the beginning of the war when German merchant ships were still at sea, and when submarines had an important part to play in contraband control, their task was largely one of endless patrolling and watching. As the war progressed submarine patrols on the lookout for surface raiders breaking out into the Atlantic increased, and were concentrated, to the submariners' great discomfort, in northern waters.

In the Mediterranean the task of the British submarines was to attack German and Italian supply lines to North Africa. The force was divided between Alexandria and Malta, and if the ten or so submarines at Malta had a richer harvest to reap, they certainly made the most of the chance. During the second half of 1941, 200,000 tons of enemy shipping were sunk, in addition to a destroyer, two torpedo boats and one submarine also sunk, as well as a battleship and two heavy cruisers damaged, for the loss of eight submarines.

Mention has been made of the difficulties and dangers experienced by convoys in the Mediterranean, especially those to Malta, which were under almost continuous bombardment from the air during daylight. There was also a constant threat to Allied naval operations from the powerful Italian fleet. However, the aggressive tactics of the British Commander-in-Chief, Admiral Cunningham, quickly established an ascendancy in morale over the Italian fleet, which was never able to exert the influence on events in the Mediterranean that its size justified. Nevertheless, the threat was real enough to remind convoys that their troubles were not necessarily confined to aircraft and submarines.

War came suddenly and brutally to the United States on 7 December 1941 when a heavily escorted force of six Japanese aircraft-carriers, 275 miles (440km) to the north of the Hawaiian Islands, launched their attack on the unsuspecting US Pacific Fleet in Pearl Harbor. The aim of this pre-emptive strike was to prevent American intervention in the planned Japanese expansion in the south-western Pacific islands. With two battleships sunk and the other six severely damaged, the raid seemed to have been a success, but there were two features of it that were to cost the Japanese dear. First, although the Pacific Fleet's battleship force was virtually destroyed, not one of its three large carriers was in Pearl Harbor at the time, and the Japanese themselves had demonstrated the importance of this new naval arm. Second, the nature of the attack had roused the government and people of the United States as nothing else could have done. The United States was not ready for war, but the events at Pearl Harbor thrust aside any possibility of doubt or apathy and left behind only a fierce determination to wreak the fullest vengeance as soon as possible.

Before Pearl Harbor, the forces of the United States Navy and the Imperial Japanese Navy were roughly equal. In capital ships Japan was at a considerable disadvantage, although she was building the two largest warships of the Second World War; to offset this the Japanese navy had six fleet carriers and four light fleet carriers with seven more (five of them large) under construction, to oppose the United States Navy's seven carriers in commission and a large number under construction. However, it must be remembered that the American forces had to be divided between two oceans, whereas the Japanese navy could concentrate in the South Pacific.

Thus the Japanese swept all before them with generally a local superiority at sea and above all total supremacy in the air. Two examples suffice. New British reinforcements in the shape of the battleship *Prince of Wales* and the battle-cruiser *Repulse* were risked when sent, without adequate air cover, to oppose Japanese landings in the northern Malay peninsula. The price was paid on 10 December 1941, both ships being caught by Japanese aircraft and sunk within ninety minutes. A few weeks later, a mixed force of cruisers and destroyers, Dutch, British, Australian and American, under the command of Admiral Doorman of the Royal Netherlands Navy, was virtually wiped out in opposing Japanese forces covering invasion convoys in the Java Sea.

The saviours of the Allied campaign in the Pacific were the US carriers which had not been caught in Pearl Harbor. It was their task, as now the backbone of the Pacific Fleet, to contain the Japanese at sea if possible, and it was appropriate that two of them, the *Lexington* and the *Enterprise*, reinforced by the carrier *Yorktown*, should play a major part in the two sea battles that halted the hitherto steady Japanese advance towards Australia.

The first of these took place in the Coral Sea during May 1942 and resulted in the Japanese recalling the convoy of transports that was to launch an amphibious attack on Port Moresby in southern New Guinea. They had lost the services of two large aircraft-carriers for some weeks, one because of damage, the other because its squadrons had been so depleted, and had also lost the smaller *Shoho* sunk. The Allied force, which included some Australian elements, suffered the loss of the fleet carrier *Lexington*, but had won a major tactical victory for the Japanese plan against Port Moresby was abandoned.

The second action, the Battle of Midway, took place a month later. The island of Midway was a crucial element in American stretegy; it was not only 1,200 miles (1,930km) nearer to the main theatre of operations than Pearl Harbor, and therefore an important base for the American submarines that were beginning to make their presence felt on the Japanese supply lines; but also by denying it to them, the Americans kept the Japanese at arm's length from the

Right, above: **HMCS *Stellarton* (1942). This type of escort vessel, a corvette, was designed to be produced in small commercial shipyards.**
Right: **HMS *Unruffled* (1943).**

central Pacific.

The Japanese motives for wanting the island were similar. In Japanese hands, together with the Aleutian Islands which were to be invaded at the same time, Midway would fend off any threat to the Japanese mainland. Admiral Yamamoto, the Japanese Commander-in-Chief and originator of the Midway plan, also hoped that by it he might force a fleet action on the Americans on terms advantageous to Japan, before the reinforcements from the American shipyards became too great.

Yamamoto sailed with the most powerful force that he could muster. With his flagship, the new 73,000-ton *Yamato,* he had ten other battleships and four carriers, as well as a large force of cruisers and destroyers, and finally the troop transports. The American force under Admiral Fletcher consisted of three carriers, eight cruisers and fourteen destroyers, with a number of submarines patrolling to the west and north of Midway. The Americans also had aircraft based on Midway.

Fortunes fluctuated considerably during the two-day battle. Fletcher had the advantage of excellent intelligence work beforehand, while Admiral Nagumo, commanding the Japanese carriers, suffered the consequences of some indifferent scouting by his reconnaissance aircraft. When Yamamoto finally called his forces off, he had lost all four carriers and a cruiser to set against the sinking of the aircraft-carrier *Yorktown.*

If the Battle of the Coral Sea caused the Japanese to pause in their advance southward, the remarkable American victory at Midway stopped dead any further movement to the north and west. Instead of pressing on with their plans, the Japanese were forced to consolidate their position. The first step was to construct an airfield on Guadalcanal in the Solomons, an island which had seen little fighting and was only lightly held. Reconnaissance reports suggested that if the Japanese were not overwhelmed quickly they might be very difficult to dislodge later. The opportunity was grasped and on 7 August 1942 American marines landed almost unopposed. The Japanese then reacted violently, however, and the island and the surrounding seas were to witness bloody battles before the last major naval encounter at the end of November and the withdrawal of the Japanese land forces in February 1943. This was achieved after months of bitter fighting at a cost, in major vessels alone, of three American aircraft-carriers, one Japanese aircraft-carrier and two Japanese battleships. On each side several cruisers and destroyers were also lost, including ships from Australia and New Zealand, and it was these lesser vessels which bore the brunt of the remainder of the fighting in the confined waters around the Solomon Islands until the Japanese were driven from the central

islands of the group in October 1943.

In all the remaining battles in the Pacific it was the Japanese who were on the defensive, desperately trying to break up invasion convoys. In the Battle of the Philippine Sea, during June 1944, American forces shot down 400 aircraft for the loss of 90 of their own; no major naval unit was sunk on either side.

The Japanese navy was finally broken in the series of four confused actions known as the Battle of Leyte Gulf from 24 to 26 October 1944. In the end the Japanese had lost three battleships, four carriers, ten cruisers and nine destroyers as well as a large proportion of the 1st and 2nd Air Fleets for which replacements, particularly in pilots, were now becoming very difficult. The United States lost one light fleet carrier and two escort carriers, and three destroyers. Nearly 200 aircraft had been lost, but at last replacements were plentiful.

While these great events had been taking place on the surface and in the air, American submarines had been drawing the strings of an ever-tightening blockade on Japan. From an indifferent performance during the Japanese advance, the submarines during 1943 became a dangerous thorn in Japan's side. In the two and a half years of the American submarine war, forty-six submarines were lost while sinking more than 1,000 ships totalling some 4,800,000 tons. In the last fourteen months of the war American submarines also accounted for two fleet carriers, two escort carriers, one battleship, two heavy cruisers, fifteen destroyers and eleven submarines.

Meanwhile, as we have seen, by the end of 1943, in European waters the Allied naval forces had succeeded in reducing the German surface fleet to one or two cruisers and some destroyers. As a result, British ships could be spared to reform the Eastern Fleet, and return to action in the Indian Ocean, where British submarines had been active since the Japanese entry into the war. Based in Ceylon, they had harassed Japanese shipping on the supply routes to Burma. Now similar operations were carried out by a fleet of battleships and aircraft-carriers, including the American carrier *Saratoga* on loan from the Pacific Fleet, with cruiser and destroyer escorts. By the end of 1944 sufficient vessels could be made available to form an East Indies Fleet and a Pacific Fleet. Accordingly in March 1945, the British Pacific Fleet under Admiral Rawlings, consisting of two modern battleships, four fleet carriers, five cruisers and ten destroyers joined the United States' Fast Carrier Force for the rest of the war.

The last two amphibious operations of the war, the assaults on Iwo Jima and Okinawa, saw the final fling of the Japanese surface forces and the greatly increased use of *kamikazes* (suicide aircraft), which had been introduced in the Battle of Leyte Gulf. Defence against

American infantry disembark from an LST (Landing Ship, Tank) in May 1944. Such vessels played a vital part in the amphibious operations so much a feature of the Second World War.

this weapon of the fanatic was very difficult, since if it was to be nullified, the diving aircraft had literally to be blown up in the air within seconds of having been spotted. The armoured flight decks of the British carriers proved their worth against the *kamikazes,* and thus suffered little damage compared with that inflicted on their American counterparts. At Iwo Jima the *Saratoga* was badly damaged by five *kamikazes* and had to return to the United States for repairs, while one suicide plane set the escort carrier *Bismarck Sea* ablaze, after which she capsized and sank.

The attack on Okinawa brought the ultimate sortie by a Japanese battleship. Much of the last oil fuel available was collected for the *Yamato,* which was sent out in April 1945 with a cruiser and destroyers to attack shipping off Okinawa. Without fighter protection, she and several of her consorts suffered the same fate as had the *Prince of Wales* and the *Repulse* off Malaya, and the battleships in Pearl Harbor. The Japanese had been the first to master the technique of the offensive use of the fleet carrier, but the Allied navies, particularly that of the United States, had learned the lesson quickly and well.

So negligible was the remaining Japanese defence in the air and in coastal waters that the Allied fleet could bombard installations on the mainland of Japan almost at will, and it was in such a bombardment of the main naval base at Kure that Japan's last two aircraft-carriers and three battleships were sunk. As a result of the atomic bombs dropped on Hiroshima and Nagasaki, the Supreme Allied Commander received the surrender of the Japanese forces on board the battleship *Missouri* on 2 September 1945.

Of the several factors that proved vital in achieving the victory at sea, three may be noticed: first, the resources of Great Britain and her Commonwealth, and of the United States of America; second, the ability of those countries to adopt and improve new techniques—the British navy, for example, in anti-submarine warfare, and the United States Navy in the tactical use of fleet carriers; and third, the wartime development of the most important single technical weapon, radar. It is significant that apart from the advantage it gave the Royal Air Force in the air battles over Britain in 1940, it also tipped the scales in the Battle of the Atlantic. In each case the enemy started well behind in maritime radar and never caught up. Similarly, in the Pacific, American forces made full use of radar, to the confusion of an enemy who was without it for most of the war.

Above: Recruits are issued with their uniform at a naval barracks in 1940. First issues were free and usually two of every piece of clothing. Later replacements were normally charged against the man's pay; some items, such as boots or, later, shoes were re-issued free for the worn-out pair. Clothing was generally of good quality, warm and hard wearing. Fitting was normally quite good, dependent perhaps upon the state of the store and the mood of the supply rating. Glaring misfits were altered by the tailor at no cost; other alterations were usually on a repayment basis. Understandably, most newly joined sailors endeavoured to get rid of their 'new boy' appearance as soon as possible, and to this end navy blue collars were often scrubbed to produce the faded look of the more seasoned hand. This sort of practice was, of course, a punishable offence since it constituted a waste of material in wartime. Authorities tended to turn a blind eye, however. One of the first things a recruit had to learn was that the navy had its own way of doing things, and woe betide the new 'OD' (seaman, Ordinary Duties) caught using any other method. In fact, although time obviously created anomalies of method, there was usually a good reason for the navy's insistence on 'the navy way'. For example, trousers were always folded with the regulation number of horizontal creases: the number for uniformity, and horizontal because it made more sense when the sailor's wardrobe was still likely to be a kit bag.

Right: A new draft for the HMS *Ark Royal* (1937), and judging from the look of the duffel coats, most of the men are newly trained recruits straight from the naval barracks. Notice the absence of large suitcases. Fixed unyielding shapes have no place on a crowded mess-deck where space of any kind is at a premium.

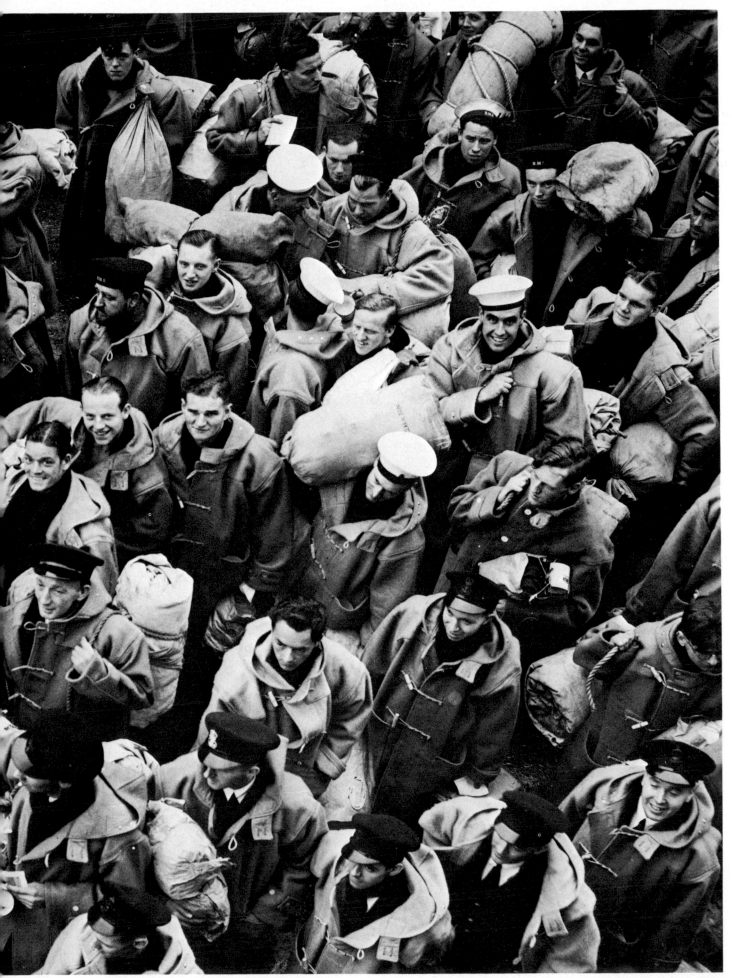

Above: Essential elements in the success of any mission are the briefing before the action and the debriefing afterwards. These two photographs taken aboard an American aircraft-carrier epitomise the difference. In the first, crews are tense, concentrating on the details of targets, duties and timing.
Above right: The second picture shows the animated nature of the debriefing session. Now it is the aircrew who do most of the talking, except for probing, analytical questions from the ship's Intelligence Officers.
Right: A third briefing photograph shows the same concentration as the first. The faces, however, are older: middle-aged Europeans, mainly British, captains of the merchant ships that will form a convoy to cross the

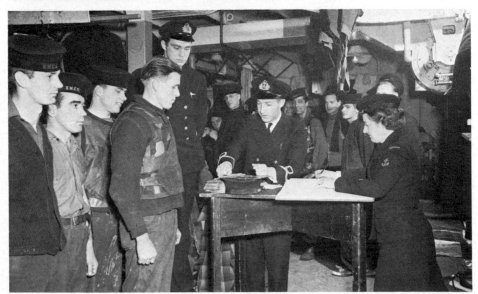

Atlantic. At the table is the commander of the escort group charged with defending the convoy, and in the last analysis, in overall command. The intertwined rings on his sleeve denote that he is a captain in the Royal Naval Reserve. In the centre of the front row sits a commander, also RNR, who as commodore of the convoy is immediately responsible for the station-keeping and discipline of merchant ships.

Left: Pay day. It is half a century from HMS *Royal Sovereign* to the HMCS *St Thomas* at St John's, Newfoundland in 1945, but despite the presence of the Leading Writer from the WRCNS instead of the bearded petty officer of 1895, the essential ingredients of this important occasion are the same.

Right: The tattered ensign flying from this escort vessel is evidence of long weeks at sea in hard weather. This particular destroyer is one of the fifty made available to Britain under the 'ships for bases' agreement. Surplus to American requirements, the destroyers were mostly twenty years old and nearly at the end of their life. They were a most useful stopgap remedy for the deficiency in escort vessels at a crucial time, however.

Below: Divine service on the fo'c's'le of the Greek cruiser *Averof* (1910).

Below right: Loading stores aboard a Romanian submarine, alongside the 'mother-ship' in a Black Sea port.

Far right: The return of the submarine HMS *Ultor* from a patrol. The 'Jolly Roger' records her successes: the stars show vessels sunk by gunfire, based on the symbol used for the Gunlayer's

badge; the bars denote ships torpedoed; the dagger indicates a secret operation, probably the landing or the collection of an agent on an enemy held shore; and the lighthouse denotes the bombardment of shore installations.

Opposite page: Morning watch aboard the Romanian destroyer *Regelé Ferdinand* (1928).

Far left: The quadruple 40mm AA guns of an American cruiser in action against a *kamikaze* aircraft. Note the concentration of each man on the job he has to do, not the approaching Japanese aeroplane.

Left, top: Preparing mines aboard an Italian mine-laying cruiser of the *Condottieri* class (1930).

Left, centre: Torpedo maintenance aboard the cruiser HMS *Sheffield* (1936) in September 1940. The censor objected to the torpedoman's pipe.

Left, bottom: The after 4-inch (100mm) guns of the *Regelé Ferdinand*. It is easy to see why the pattern of depth-charge thrower shown in the picture was known as the 'coal scuttle' type.

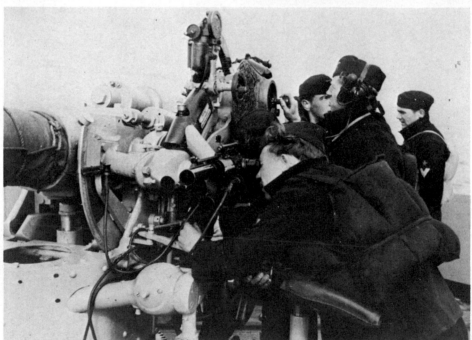

Top: The Italian battleship *Vittorio Veneto* (1937) using her main armament of 16-inch (406mm) guns in the action of Cape Matapan on 28 March 1941. The Italian fleet constituted a grave threat to Allied convoys in the Mediterranean Sea and was only kept subdued by the vigorous aggressive tactics of Admiral Cunningham, Commander-in-Chief of the British Mediterranean Fleet, and his successors. Matapan was a severe defeat for Italy.

Above: Minesweeping was one of the less pleasant jobs during the war on either side. The vessels were at sea in all weathers; they were generally slow and uncomfortable; they could not run away from anything when attacked, yet their own armament was so small that it afforded little protection and could drive off only the most half-hearted of attacks from the air. With all this were the ever-present dangers inherent in their unenviable task. The photograph shows the gun crew of a German

minesweeper in August 1942. The man nearest the camera is using a range-finder; next to him is the communications number.
Right: Almost as dangerous was the work of preparing and laying mines, although minelayers generally had the advantage of being regular warships, faster and better armed than minesweepers. The photograph shows two German sailors with a rather grim sense of humour, 'Roses from the South' being a popular 1930s waltz.

Early on the morning of Sunday 7 December 1941 Japanese aircraft dived out of the sky upon the unsuspecting United States naval base at Pearl Harbor. There had been no declaration of war, and certainly the attack was unprovoked; nevertheless there had been a steady deterioration in Japanese-American relations although talks were taking place as the Japanese sought to allay American suspicions. They were successful in achieving surprise. A report of a fleet of aeroplanes approaching was dismissed as probably being a squadron of Flying Fortresses expected in from the mainland. In one important respect the United States was lucky, for while Japanese aircraft wreaked havoc among the battleships and cruisers, their primary targets, the fleet carriers *Saratoga, Lexington* and *Enterprise,* were not there.

Left: An airfield during the attack, with smoke from burning oil tanks billowing in the background.

Below: The action which brought the first check to the Japanese advance southward, the Battle of the Coral Sea, saw the loss of the *Lexington,* one of the carriers 'missed' at Pearl Harbor. Survivors are here being pulled aboard a rescue ship, still moving slowly because a stationary target is too easy a mark for submarines.

Below: Russian forces at sea were negligible during the Second World War. The picture shows the destroyer *Karl Marx* (1914) caught by German dive bombers and left a burned out wreck.

Above: In the galley aboard HMCS *Agassiz* in 1941. The seaman receiving the soup is in the galley solely for the purposes of the photograph; his entry would normally have received a sharp response from the petty officer.

Right, above: 'Splicing the main brace' aboard HMCS *Arvid* to celebrate the surrender of Italy, 1943. In the days of sail, if the main brace parted in a gale and had to be spliced together again, still in bad weather, it was a very arduous and unpleasant job. Because of this it was the custom to make a special issue of rum as a reward, and probably a reviver. Thus the term 'splice the main brace' became associated with the issue of an extra tot. A tradition that survived until 1970 in the British and Commonwealth navies, the tot of rum issued each forenoon to all ratings over the age of 18 was in fact half a gill of rum and water. The addition of water served

two purposes: it diluted the rum and, perhaps more important, made it impossible to keep for long, so that the men could not bottle it. The tot, carefully measured out by a petty officer under the eye of the Officer of the Watch, was treasured by all who drew it. It was often the currency for bets, frequently concerning the accuracy of a rumour or 'buzz'. The payment took one of three forms: 'sippers', when the victor acknowledged his right with a sip; a man with great faith in his story might stake 'gulpers', a good swallow, on it; on 'dead certs' a whole tot has been staked and lost, although on such occasions the full penalty was not always exacted.

Right, below: Mid-afternoon in the stokers' mess aboard HMCS *Kamsack*: tea with tinned/canned evaporated milk, poured through holes punched with a knife or marlin-spike.

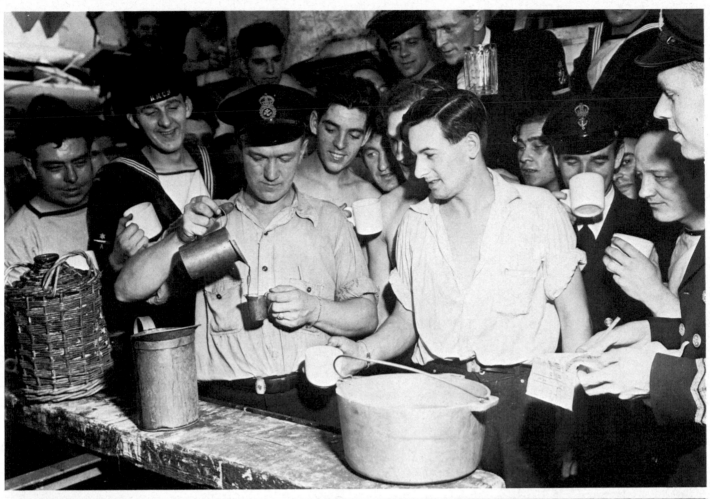

Right: Aboard the Free French destroyer *La Triomphante* (1934), *matelots* line up for the issue of *vin rouge* for their respective messes.
Below: Not potatoes this time, but runner beans by the thousand, aboard a British cruiser in 1943.
Bottom: On a German 'E' boat returning from patrol, a seaman makes his precarious way across the deck with mugs and a jug of boiling hot coffee.
Far right: In the petty officers' mess in a British submarine.

Left: American pilots on stand-by relax in the 'Ready Room' on board an aircraft-carrier. On the bulkhead by the door is an identification poster showing the Japanese 'Zero' fighter.

Above: These sailors, aboard a ship in the British Home Fleet, write letters home one evening in 1943. Photographs of wives and girlfriends are brought out to make the link with home more tangible. Tucked in the edge of a drawer by the rack for the cases, the picture of 'Uncle Joe' Stalin had no political significance during the war. The smiling 'father-figure' image was accepted at its face value, part of the propaganda to ensure a united front against the common enemy.

Below: In the ship's canteen, 'Jack' could buy luxuries (or necessities, depending on one's priorities) which made life more pleasant. The barrels and the crates contain beer, but no hard liquors were available. Profits from the canteen went into the Ship's Fund, which was used for functions that benefited everyone, a film show or a dance perhaps, and was administered by a committee of all ranks. Note the emergency lighting. The man at the hatch is probably just going ashore since he is wearing his hat and carrying his gas-mask.

Right, above: Four sailors of the United States Coast Guard, which provided the US Navy with reserves and crews for landing-craft, in a dance-hall in Britain.

Right, below: Sailors in the canteen of a former ocean liner turned into a depot ship. They are playing a form of Ludo called 'Uckers' which vied with tombola (bingo) as the most popular pastime on the crowded mess-decks.

Far right: Everybody's picture of a sailor home from the sea: kitbag on his shoulder, exotic present for wife or mother in hand, a smile on his face and a jaunty step. This young sailor is seen leaving Euston Station.

Left, above: A U-boat commander in the fifth year of the war. The signs of strain caused by dangerous patrols can be seen in the face.

Left, below: Oberleutnant Gerd Schaar, a holder of the Knight's Cross, congratulates a newly decorated man.

Right, top: Three young men are inspected by the commanding officer of an officer's school in northern Germany. They have been recommended for commissions following outstanding service in action.

Right, centre: Before the assembled ship's company on the flight-deck of an American aircraft-carrier, Admiral Chester Nimitz reads the citation before presenting the Navy Cross to Steward Doris Miller.

Right, bottom: Recipients of the Distinguished Service Medal at Buckingham Palace in May 1942, Petty Officer H. Fright and Able Seaman J. Shanahan seem to typify the navy's link with the past. The Royal Navy has special rules about beards: no one may grow just a beard or only a moustache. A sailor must grow a 'full set' or remain clean-shaven. Good Conduct Badges, the chevrons worn on the left arm, are awarded petty officers and ratings at the completion of three, eight and thirteen years. On the mess-deck during the Second World War, when men were frequently rated Leading Seaman with less than three years service, the 'Badgie' sometimes had more influence than the Leading Hand because of his experience.

Below: U-boat ace *Korvettenkapitän* Schütze and his crew are wished good luck as they prepare to set out on another patrol.

Right: Italian seamen roll up an anti-submarine net used for harbour defence.

Right, centre: With ice on his sou'wester and his shoulders, this picture of a U-boat commander typifies the problems posed to men in the navies of both sides who fought in northern waters. The common enemy was the weather. Overnight, rigging could become inches thick with frozen spray. ice had to be chipped off frequently because if it was allowed to accumulate, the enormous weight so high above the ship's centre of gravity could make her unstable. Often, of course, this particular hazard was also made worse by gales. Men dreaded being swept overboard, for apart from the difficulty of being picked up again, there was the certainty that a man in the water would not last more than five or six minutes because of the cold.

Right, bottom: Mechanics in the engine room of a U-boat. The submarines of both world wars used diesel engines for their power on the surface and electric motors when submerged. This system required an enormous weight of lead-acid storage batteries, but still gave the submarine only a limited period submerged before she had to surface and recharge her batteries with the diesel engines. It was the need to use electric motors when submerged that so drastically limited the submarine's speed under water. This type of vessel should more properly be called a submersible rather than a submarine since it is really a surface vessel with the ability to run submerged for a limited period.

Far right: The Leading Signalman repairing a signal flag in the picture would have been known in the jargon of the lower deck as a Leading (or sometimes Killick) Bunting-tosser. The term Killick for Leading Seaman comes from the old name for an anchor, which was his badge of rank worn on the left arm. His trade qualification was shown by crossed flags on his right arm. He is standing on the signal bridge of a destroyer awaiting the order to hoist and break out the flag already attached to the signal halliard.

140

CHAPTER 5
POST-1945

T he period since 1945 has been as complex as that leading to 1914, and the technological revolution has been even greater. The balance of power at sea has also shifted considerably. A fluctuating economy has reduced the British navy to one of the second rank in size, whilst the navy of the Soviet Union, negligible during the Second World War, now rivals that of the United States.

The two most important technological innovations have been nuclear power and rocket missiles, which have made the nuclear submarine the modern equivalent of the capital ship.

In 1945, the only major fleets of the world belonged to Great Britain and the United States of America, that of the latter being considerably larger. In order to cut defence costs, however, the British government of the day drastically reduced the Royal Navy. Despite this, it was in the Royal Navy that many of the notable improvements to conventional ships appeared: the gas turbine engine, the steam catapult and the mirror landing device among others.

First perfected in its marine form by Rolls Royce in the early 1950s, the gas turbine engine has the advantage that not only does it generate more power than a steam turbine of the same size, but it can also produce that power immediately. The gas turbine is commonly used in conjunction with either the steam turbine or diesel engines, the latter being used for cruising, and the gas turbine for emergencies and high-speed work.

The steam catapult, considerably more powerful than any hydraulic catapult then in use, was first introduced in the *Ark Royal* in 1955, and was quickly adopted by the United States Navy and others.

Although first used in service by the United States Navy, the idea of the angled deck was first conceived in Britain in 1951. The introduction of the angled deck solved a problem so basic to the operation of aircraft-carriers that it is surprising that neither the Americans nor the Japanese had hit upon it earlier. The forward part of the flight deck of a carrier has at times to act as an aircraft park. Consequently any aircraft that missed the arrester wires on landing had to be stopped by a barrier before it ran into the parked aircraft, an expensive and barely satisfactory solution. If the pilot were to land on a deck angled away from the ship's longitudinal axis, however, and miss the arrester wires, he could accelerate and take off again without danger to the other machines.

Trials made with an angled deck painted on the

Left: **Newly commissioned young officers of the Israeli navy in high spirits immediately following their graduation parade at Haifa 15 June 1970.**
Above: **Sailors in the East Germany navy on parade.**

143

British carrier *Triumph* were immediately successful, as were others similarly carried out on the American carrier *Midway* a few weeks later.

The first angled-deck carrier in service was the US *Antietam,* which was converted by the end of 1952. The first British angled deck carrier was the *Ark Royal,* completed in 1955. Under construction when the tests were carried out, the *Ark Royal* was altered to include the new feature, which immediately became part of the standard aircraft-carrier design.

The mirror landing aid, introduced in 1955, gives the pilot of an approaching aircraft a visual image of his position relative to the carrier deck, a far more accurate method that that which needed a landing signals officer (batsman) who guides the pilot in by waving a pair of coloured paddles. Again, the system was adopted by other navies as carriers were built.

Aircraft-carriers have become ever larger, partly because of the increased size and speed of the aircraft, partly of course to enable them to carry more aircraft for longer periods at sea. The American carriers of the *Forrestal* class, termed 'super-carriers' when laid down in 1952, are over 1,000 feet (304.8m) long with a displacement of 54,000 tons. They were the first carriers designed to take jet aircraft. The latest American carriers are nuclear powered with a displacement of more than 75,000 tons. They can carry 90 per cent more aviation fuel than the *Forrestal* class, and 50 per cent more ammunition.

The United States is the only country that has built any large aircraft-carriers for some years. The new carriers built for other navies have been smaller versions for use with helicopters and aircraft of the Harrier type, requiring little distance for landing.

The introduction of missiles has turned upside down the picture of a battleship with eight or ten mighty guns with barrels 60 feet (18.3m) long. The most powerful surface vesseels afloat are the guided-missile cruisers, with a strike capability far greater than that of any battleship ever built. The guided missile has given the modern frigate and destroyer a firepower greater than that of any heavy cruiser of 1944. The modern capital ship, the nuclear-powered submarine, while still submerged, can attack a target far away.

In January 1955 the American *Nautilus* put to sea. It was the first nuclear-powered ship, and the first true submarine: a vessel designed to cruise below the surface of the sea, as opposed to her forerunners who could submerge as required, but for strictly limited periods. The *Nautilus* was designed as an attack or fleet submarine, with the capability of seeking and destroying other submarines. In that sense her armament is conventional.

In 1959 the United States Navy commissioned the *George Washington,* the first of five submarines that were not only nuclear-powered, but were also armed with the Polaris ballistic missile. This class was adapted from an attack design, but since the last of them was put into service in 1961, the United States Navy has built thirty-five more even larger submarines of the *Ethan Allen* and the *Lafayette* classes, capable of firing the improved Poseidon missile. The United States Navy now has well over one hundred nuclear submarines of all types. There are also under construction the first four of ten 16,000-ton nuclear submarines, capable of firing 24 Trident missiles which have a range of 4,000 miles (6,440km).

The Soviet Union started to build nuclear submarines in 1958. These were armed with conventional weapons, but others soon followed with cruise missiles (surface to surface). The first Soviet nuclear-powered submarine armed with ballistic missiles appeared in 1962, since when the Soviet Union has indulged in something of a 'race' with the United States in the production of these vessels.

Great Britain experimented with submarines powered by hydrogen peroxide in 1955 as a cheaper alternative to nuclear power. Unfortunately the boats were not a success. In 1960 the *Dreadnought,* a fleet boat and the Royal Navy's first nuclear submarine, was launched, and eleven similar craft have followed. Between 1967 and 1969 Britain's four nuclear missile submarines were completed.

The French navy is gradually being rebuilt, but it suffers from the fact that France has traditionally looked first and foremost to her army for defence, with the navy being granted only a very secondary role. Surrounded now by friendly countries, the nuclear defence of France lies chiefly with the navy.

In the French navy, that submarine missile deterrent was developed rather differently. The submarine *Gymnote,* conventionally powered but armed with ballistic missiles, was completed in 1963. The first French nuclear submarine was *La Redoutable,* which became operational in 1971. France now has five similar vessels all armed with strategic ballistic missiles. All the French attack submarines are conventionally powered. In surface vessels, her two carriers are supported by guided-missile cruisers and destroyers.

The Royal Netherlands Navy has no nuclear-powered vessels. Its main force lies with its guided-missile destroyers and its conventionally powered attack submarines.

West Germany, too, has guided-missile destroyers and a number of conventional submarines of the attack type.

Modern torpedoes are vastly superior to those used in the Second World War. They carry a more powerful warhead and are wire-guided until close enough for their own mechanism to 'home them in' on a heat source such as a ship's engines.

One significant development from the use of missiles

The *Marshal Voroshilov*, a Russian guided-missile cruiser of the *Kresta* class (1965).

is that lesser countries who can, as in the past, afford only small craft, can wield a power off their own coast out of all proportion to the size of the navy. For missiles, unlike the heavy guns of forty years ago, do not need huge platforms. The small but efficient Israeli navy, for example, is a potent force at the eastern end of the Mediterranean. The importance of electronics has increased enormously, not only with radar and navigation, but more crucially in weapon control.

Conditions have changed on board ship, too, especially in the nuclear submarines. Accommodation in these ships, which average about 7,500 tons, is no longer cramped as in submarines of the past. The possibility of nuclear attack warfare has imposed another condition on modern warships: they must be capable of being worked and fought while totally sealed off from the outside world and radio-activity.

Left: Israeli frogmen armed with automatic rifles cast off in their inflatable assault craft to land on a 'hostile' beach during an exercise in July 1969.

Top: Part of the crew of a Russian-built *Shershen* class (c1966) torpedo boat of the East German navy. The engineer, a warrant officer, is on the left. The captain is wearing the headset.

Above: An Alouette III helicopter landing at an airfield. The Alouette III is carried on board the French frigates of the E-50 and E-52 types for anti-submarine work. it is also widely used as a search and rescue, and general utility machine.

Top: Volunteers for the new navy of the German Federal Republic (West Germany) report for duty at Wilhelmshaven naval base on 1 January 1956.
Above: Three days later they are on parade, smartly turned out, ready for inspection by the commanding officer, *Kapitän* Reschke.
Above, right: West German sailors on an electronics course. The instructor is describing the function of new equipment they may later be required to handle during their service.

Right: In recent years the United States Navy has carried out a programme of investigations into the use of dolphins, porpoises and whales in certain branches of naval intelligence. In the Pacific Ocean, a member of the Deep Operations Recovery System team gives a fish snack to a pilot whale swimming alongside a motor boat. The whale is trained to make deep ocean recoveries of such objects as experimental torpedoes and other inert test ordnance.

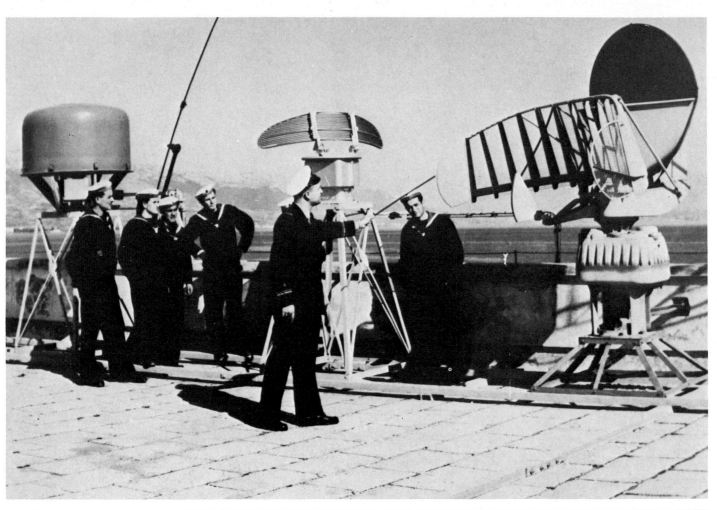

Left: Until the end of the war diving was carried out by men in the traditional heavy suits, with weighted boots and a helmet fed by an airline. This sort of diving severely limited the operations that could be performed. The development of the aqua-lung in use towards the end of the war and the freedom of movement it has accorded the diver has revolutionised diving. No longer is a boat capable of carrying a heavy air-compressor required. Divers can now use the light and manoeuvrable inflatable dinghy as a safety vessel on the spot, with the headquarters vessel farther away if necessary. However, the free diver is not confined to salvage or repair work, but can now be used in an offensive role. The appearance of the diver prompted the term 'frogman', an apt if unflattering description. The photograph shows Israeli frogmen during a training exercise in Haifa Bay in February 1970.

Right, above: Seamen line up on the deck of the Israeli submarine *Dolphin* (1944) after completing their training course. The *Dolphin* is a British 'T' class submarine (formerly HMS *Truncheon*), rebuilt for the Israeli navy in 1966. It has been modified for the transport of frogmen for commando operations and is also used for training purposes.

Right, centre: Aboard the aircraft-carrier USS *Lexington* (ex-*Cabot*, 1942) in the pleasant waters of the Gulf of Mexico, a naval airman instructs midshipmen from a private Naval and Military Academy. The midshipmen are on their annual two-week Active Duty training course in October 1968.

Right, below: Duty crewmen in the control room of a French submarine of the *Narval* class (1957-60).

Left: In this striking photograph two members of the crew of the destroyer tender USS *Sierra* (1944) wash down the paint work on her bows.

Top: In HMS *Phoenix*, a naval shore establishment, officers and ratings are taught fire-fighting as part of damage-control techniques. The picture shows a seaman, wearing a fire-resistant suit and breathing apparatus, tackling a blaze with a foam jet.

Above: The two Russian sailors practise damage-control methods. In their case the enemy is not fire but water, gushing through a hole that might have been caused by a near miss. Damage control is of great importance in all warships, and well repays conscientious training. Many ships have been lost as a result of poor damage control planning.

Far left, above: With the reduction of
the Royal Navy in the years following
the end of the Second World War,
efforts were made to retain useful ships
in reserve without incurring expensive
maintenance costs. The chief
requirement was to seal all vital
machinery and moving parts from
moisture, and this produced the effect
of the huge silvery white 'cocoons'.
First, however, every vestige of rust
had to be removed from all metalwork.
The photograph shows a party at work
with electric hammers and grinders
doing the work that was formerly
carried out by a large number of sailors
with chipping hammers—but doing it
not only faster, but far more efficiently.
Far left, below: The cruiser HMCS
Ontario (1943) was presented to
Canada by the British government on
her completion in 1945. The picture
shows an ERA (engine room articifer)

explaining the use of a lathe.
Left: A Chinese naval sentry at the
naval base at the former British treaty
port of Wei-hai-wei. The Chinese navy
contains at least one nuclear submarine
of the 'attack' type, of Russian design
as are most of her warships,
dating from the period of co-operation
between the two countries.
Above: A signalman of the Yugoslav
navy, photographed during an exercise
in 1972. The *Mornar* (1958) is a patrol
boat of the French *Foug eux* class,
built in Yugoslavia. Of the European
powers, France has excelled in the
design and production of small, fast
patrol boats for export to countries
without the resources for larger
warships. Indeed, the missile-armed
patrol boat is perhaps superior to
larger warships in restricted waterssuch
as in the eastern end of the
Mediterranean.

Left: American seamen prepare to use an electric winch aboard the USS *William C. Lawe* (1945) prior to coming alongside a jetty at the Pensacola naval base in Florida. The traditional dress of the seaman, almost international as a uniform for over a hundred years and based on a lineage far more ancient, has been discarded for work on deck. Overalls are more convenient, as are the 'baseball' type hats. Heavy work gloves also prevent minor injuries to the hands. An old-style martinet petty officer would no doubt find one major fault with the overalls—they have pockets! Modern warships use so much complex equipment, of an order far higher than that used in the Second World War, that the provision of sensible clothing and creative comforts is essential for the efficiency of all navies.
Below: Yugoslavian mechanics under training study a diesel engine. Equipment in the Yugoslav navy has varied sources: British and American engines (note the Evinrude outboard motor), Swedish weapons, and French- and Russian-designed vessels.

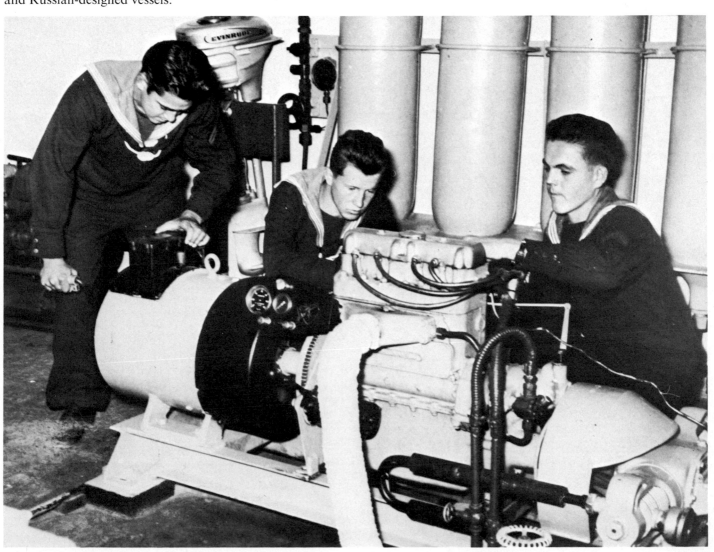

Above: The Israeli navy concentrates most of its power in fast patrol boats armed with missiles. The photograph, taken in 1970, shows a French-built *Saar* class (1969) gunboat. She carries eight missile-launchers, the pod of one of the triple set amidships being open and the missile visible. The Israeli-designed Gabriel missile system is a highly sophisticated surface to surface weapon with a range of about 6 miles (10km) and a 165-lb (75kg) warhead of conventional explosive.

Left: One of the last of the conventional warships in the French navy, the destroyer *Surcouf* was present for a naval exhibition in Paris in September 1956. The two sailors in the photograph are polishing the muzzles of two 5-in (127mm) guns.

Right: The American heavy cruiser *Boston* (1942) was re-equipped with Terrier missiles in the 1950s. The photograph shows a missile mounting captain standing by to fire during an exercise in May 1962. The helmet appears too large, but contains a lot of communications gear.

159

Left: The essence of efficiency in any armed service lies in discipline; to this end there is still much to be gained from a certain amount of drill which, if it does nothing else, teaches the habit of obedience to words of command. The photograph shows recruits in the Kenyan navy undergoing some old-fashion 'square-bashing'. The Kenyan navy's fleet consists of a number of coastal patrol boats.

Above: West German sailors man their vessel, a submarine, at the beginning of a training exercise.

Right: An Ikara missile and torpedo in its launcher, on board the Australian guided-missile destroyer HMAS *Perth* (1963). The Ikara is an anti-submarine weapon system designed and developed in Australia. It has also been adopted by the Royal Navy for some of its destroyers and frigates. An indication of the bulk of modern missile systems may be seen in the relative sizes of the launcher complex and the man standing beside it. Relatively few 'reloads' can be carried.

Left: Midget submarines for the Royal Navy were developed for the attack on the German battleship *Tirpitz* as she lay in the shelter of a Norwegian fjord. The picture shows the *X-51*, a midget submarine introduced into service in 1954. Standing on deck, left to right, are Chief ERA Barker, Lieutenant J.R. Midgely, the captain, and his first lieutenant, Lieutenant Strang.

Above: By contrast with the *X-51* and even with the U-boat engine room shown on page 140, the inside of a nuclear submarine is huge. The picture shows a torpedo rating in the torpedo-room of HMS *Resolution*, Britain's first Polaris missile nuclear submarine. The hinged circular hatches on the right are for the loading of torpedoes. It is first checked that the bow caps, which open to allow the torpedo to be fired from the tube into the water, are closed, and then these inner hatches may be opened, the torpedos inserted, the hatches reclosed and all prepared for firing.

Right: Sailors of the German Democratic Republic (East Germany) parade as their flagship, the *Ernest Thaelmann*, comes alongside on the 150th anniversary of the birth of Fredrich Engels, and is given the name as an honorary distinction.

Left: Thai sailors enjoying the ride in a dodgem car during leave whilst visiting Great Britain for the Coronation Review of the Fleet on 15 June 1953. Thailand's navy consists largely of anti-submarine vessels and patrol boats, many of them dating from the late 1960s. The flagship is the guided-missile frigate *Makut Rajakumaru,* built in 1971.

Above: Two Italian sailors on the way back to their ship, the square-rigged training vessel *Amerigo Vespucci.* The occasion was also the Coronation Review, but look at those stores!

Right: Two sailors from Sri Lanka aboard their minesweeper at the time of the Coronation Review.

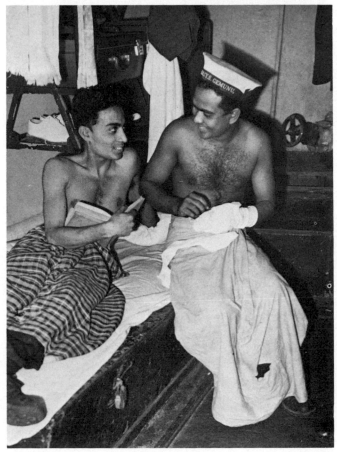

Far left: The Norwegian destroyer *Bergen* (1945) built as a 'C' class destroyer for the Royal Navy, seen in the Pool of London above Tower Bridge in August 1951. The *Bergen* was on a training cruise, and her captain hit upon a novel idea to encourage a competitive spirit between the two forward 4.5-inch (114-mm) gun turrets: 'A' turret was named Donald Duck, 'B' turret Popeye the Sailor. Three young sailors stand by their turret which has Donald Duck complete with headphones, painted on the side, reporting himself 'clear'.

Left, above: Danish sailors from the guided-missile patrol boat *Fyen* (1962), part of a squadron on a goodwill visit to London in 1966. The *Fyen*, numbered N 81, is in the background. In 1976 the Royal Danish Navy was based on a nucleus of six modern conventional submarines, a number of missile frigates and twenty guided-missile patrol boats and conventional torpedo boats for coastal work.

Left, below: One of the cooks aboard the Russian guided-missile destroyer *Obraztsovy,* of the *Kashin* class (1963-66). To anyone thinking in the conventional terminology, destroyer is something of a misnomer for this type of warship. Displacing about 5,000 tons, the average modern destroyer is nearly as big as a Second World War light cruiser with a much greater and more accurate hitting power.

Left: For the first time for more than a hundred years, wives and families sailed with their menfolk aboard a British warship in July 1956. The warship was the cruiser HMS *Tyne*, flagship of the Home Fleet, and the reason was to encourage family interest in the navy. The voyage was not far—roughly 20 miles (32km)—from Southampton to Portsmouth, but it gave the visitors an opportunity to see something of life afloat. The photograph shows a smartly turned out young electrician, 'wires' to his friends, and his wife by the rail as the *Tyne* makes her way slowly down Southampton Water.

Above: A much younger visitor is also shown off to messmates, this time by a proud father.

The varying nature of a sailor's interests are well illustrated on these pages; and diverse they are, for no one should really believe that Russian sailors spend all their spare time writing poetry, any more than British sailors do nothing but chat up the local girls or that North Koreans spend all their off-duty hours singing.

Left, above: The North Koreans are evidently enjoying the climax of their performance on a patrol boat.

Left, below: On a more intellectual plane, the Russian submariners seem to be enjoying the verses, patriotic no doubt.

Right, above: The private joke shared in the evening sunshine took place at Gibraltar early in 1952.

Right below: The four Israeli sailors on the mess-deck of a patrol boat are intent on a type of backgammon.

Top: On board the Portuguese navy's sail training ship, the three-masted barque *Sagres,* cadets dance to an accordion. The occasion was a visit to Portsmouth in August 1954.
Above: Different entertainment is found on the Rieperbahn in Hamburg by sailors from the Royal Netherlands Navy's missile cruiser *De Zeven Provincien* in 1957. The girls' 'sailor's dance' might have been neither authentic in origin nor precise in execution, but it was obviously popular with the Dutch audience.
Right: On a visit to Split by HMS *Liverpool,* flagship of the Mediterranean Fleet in 1951, a rating seeks less energetic pleasures, and is content with Yugoslavian beer and the Adriatic sunshine.

Left, above: 'I'm just a simple sailor' is a phrase often heard from both officers and men from the navies of Great Britain, the United States, Sweden, France and no doubt other nations, and it is rarely, if ever, quite the whole truth. Only a few sailors, of whatever rank, would claim to be intellectuals, however, so that one must view with some suspicion the ostentation of the captain of a Russian guided-missile destroyer playing chess against six members of his crew simultaneously— and no doubt winning.

Right, above: More readily believable is the picture of Russian sailors enjoying the sight of their ship's mascot drinking milk from a tin.

Left, below: The remaining two pictures present an amusing contrast. The sailor enjoying the mildly salacious entertainment in the Suiza Bar in Gibraltar are all mature men, most of them knowledgeable in the ways of the world and wise in the ways of the navy. The able seaman leaning on the stage for example has been 'in' for at least five years.

Right, below: The two very young men with lemonade and cakes are not yet ready for such pleasures and are only just ready for the navy. They are new cadets seen in the canteen of the *Britannia* Royal Naval College in October 1946, members of the first 'term' of cadets back at Dartmouth after the war. Thirteen years old, they will spend three and a half years in *Britannia* before going to sea as midshipment until they pass their examinations for promotion to sub-lieutenant. The Royal Navy broke with tradition in the 1970s when the age for admission to the Royal Naval College at Dartmouth was raised to sixteen and a half. The cadet now leaves the college a sub-lieutenant at the age of twenty, and the rank of midshipman has finally been discontinued.

Roxby Press Productions wish to thank the following individuals
and organizations for permission to reproduce illustrations
appearing in the book:
The Australian News Service, London; The Bettman Archive, New
York; Department of the Navy, Washington; Europa GmbH,
Munich; Den Helder Naval Museum, Netherlands; Imperial War
Museum, London; IBA International Bilderagentur, Zurich; Israel
Information, London; The Jewish Observer, London; London
Editions, London; The Mansell Collection, London;
Marinemuseet, Horten; Marine Nationale SIRPA, France; J. G.
Moore, London; Museo Naval, Montalban, Madrid; Museo Naval,
Milan; National Maritime Agency, London; Orlogsmuseet,
Copenhagen; Pathe Film Library, London; Popperfoto, London;
Public Archives of Canada, Ottawa; Radio Times Hulton Picture
Library, London; Robert Hunt Library, London; H. Roger-Viollet,
Paris; Snark International, Paris; Statens Sjohistoriska Museum,
Stockholm.